2/2

The Me

MW00638511

Zed –

That to see
you!

Happy Day –

Josh Doth

The Memory Bank

BY

JACK ORTH

www.bookstandpublishing.com

Published by
Bookstand Publishing
Morgan Hill, CA 95037
3351_4

ISBN 978-1-58909-936-4

Printed in the United States of America

PREFACE

At some time in our lives, if we're lucky enough to hit senior citizen status, there seems to be a certain age when you begin to make withdrawals from your Memory Bank on a regular basis. When you're young, maybe three or four-years-old, you open your account at the Memory Bank with your first deposit and visit the institution often over the next sixty or seventy years.

For some reason we leave the memories in that vault gaining interest for years without drawing them out. When I was a kid, my mother and father said on occasion, "Jack, whenever you get a few pennies or more, it just burns a hole in your pocket, and you have to take it out and spend it. You should save some for a rainy day." Well, I saved a lot of memories and when I retired in 1998, I began withdrawing them on a regular basis – on rainy days – sunny days, and it didn't matter, The Bank was always open!

For me, the seventy-year-old mark was the magic number. It was as though the president of The Bank called me and said my account was overloaded, and I'd have to start making withdrawals! It's been going on now for ten years, and I sure hope it continues for another ten at least.

You may relate to some of my withdrawals, and want to rush to The Bank and withdraw some of your own. I hope so, because if you do, you'll have as much fun as I've had writing a few of my own! You'll notice I said "writing," because if *I* typed them the book wouldn't be published for at least another ten years! My wife, Sally, and our good friends, Barbara Deckman and Tracy Walters, came through for me with typing and editing.

One of the nice things about memories is that only the good ones seem to gain interest in The Bank! Thanks for listening and reading.

Table of Contents

NURSERY SCHOOL

All of us have an account in the Memory Bank, and with all the banks that I've dealt with over the years, the Memory Bank is by far my favorite. There are no fees, minimum balances, or late charges…and as Master Card states in their commercials, "The interest rates are priceless!"

My account was opened in 1931, in Boston, Massachusetts, where I was born. However, the first couple of years' deposits are in a safe deposit box gaining interest, but I'm unable to withdraw them because I just plain can't remember them! But I do have memorable deposits that I fall back on beginning around 1934. I drew an "oldie" out the other day as I was leaving Mayport Elementary School. I read for kindergarten classes for an hour or two each week, and that wonderful endeavor always opens The Bank.

I whooshed back in time to Hingham, Massachusetts, and could see, just as plain as day, the nursery school on Main Street about a mile away from our house. My sister, Ann, was in first grade, and I was in nursery school in the same building. My deposits in the Memory Bank regarding nursery school weren't good ones, but no one ever guaranteed that every deposit would be perfect.

My main complaint each day to my mother was that the teacher constantly rang a little bell at school, which meant a different activity would now begin. Just when one was becoming enthralled with, let's say, drawing a picture of your favorite animal, you'd hear the tinkle of the little bell…it's time for a nap, or it's time for something else. This happened all the time, and within days, caused tears to run down my face each morning when facing another trip to hear the bell ringers.

It was too regimented for me, I guess. In a flash one morning, my mother once again did something that endeared her to me, and she continued that trait all her life.

"Jack, I think you'll be able to progress in life without the addition of nursery school and the 'bell ringers.' We'll prepare you for first grade here at home."

That may not be exactly how she announced the news to me, but that's what it said on the withdrawal slip…and I'm sticking with it. All I know is that I was one happy kid!

Years later, in the 1960s, our daughter, Wendy, entered nursery school. My wife, Sally, or I drove her each day to the place of learning in Oakland, New Jersey. My job transfer to New York brought us to the area. Each day, Wendy's lips would quiver a little, and a tear or two would appear at the thought of another day of nursery school.

I pulled into the school parking lot to drop her off, and just before a goodbye hug, I heard the distant ringing of the bells!

"Wendy, I think you'll be able to progress in life without the addition of nursery school. We'll prepare you for first grade at home!"

Wendy was one happy ex-nursery school attendee, and Sally and I had given her something nice to put in her Memory Bank!

So…draw something out of your account today, and sit back and enjoy it!

THE SWAN BOATS

Whether you're a three-year-old kid, or an eighty-five-year-old kid, you have to go for a ride on the Swan Boats when you're in Boston. They've been around since the 1870s, and I hope the Paget Family continues to set sail in the pond at the Public Gardens from April to September for another hundred years!

When my sister, Ann, and I were three or four years old, my mother would walk us down Charles Street from West Cedar Street and head for the Swan Boats! They're the same now as they were in 1934, when we first rode in them. The small, barge-like boat with eight or so rows of high back benches, and the great Swan in the back would greet us every few weeks for our cruise on the pond – all of fifteen minutes on the pond, but the memories have lasted a lifetime!

The captain of the boat would sit inside the huge Swan, and peddle the boat like a bicycle on the wonderful cruise. Generations of Bostonians have taken that ride, and I for one, never get sick of withdrawing that memory from The Bank.

We'd cross the street to the Boston Common and walk over to the Frog Pond, and hopefully once in awhile go to Bailey's for the most wonderful chocolate sundae in America! Of course the Depression was in full swing, so Bailey's was only visited now and then. That even made it more of a treat.

In later years, we took our own kids on the Swan Boats, and then over to Bailey's or Brigham's for the same wonderful surprises we had years before. Then, when they got a little older we might even take them to the Ritz Carlton, right across from the Public Gardens for lunch!

I guess my favorite story about the Swan Boats happened in later years. One of the advertising sales guys in the Fairchild Publications office, Paul Lee, with *Women's Wear Daily* actually made money by taking clients on the Swan Boats. One year he approached some of the advertising agency people he worked with, and suggested they take a cruise on his yacht and to have lunch!

They, of course, jumped at the chance to cruise on Paul's boat, and figured they'd be heading out in Boston Harbor for lunch. Paul took them on the Swan Boats and then to lunch at the Ritz. Well, it became an annual cruise for Paul and his agency, and that little investment put a lot of money in Paul's pocket due to increased advertising.

You know, I've found when I make withdrawals from my Memory Bank that I deposited way back when, they gain in stature. They've been tucked away, and when you take them out, they give you so much pleasure that you want to go back to The Bank more often.

The Swan Boats do that for me. The Paget family may not realize that over the years millions and millions of people deposited those wonderful memories in their Bank. I've never met any of the Pagets, but I salute them for creating something nice for so many people!

THE GREAT DEPRESSION

From 1929 to 1939, the Great Depression hung, like the black cloud it was, over the United States. In later years, children born during that time frame received the title of "Depression Kids." My sister, Ann, was born in 1930, I was born in 1931, and Julie was born in 1937. However, all the deposits in my Memory Bank during that time frame have no asterisk by them that classified them as Depression years. In later years, we found out how difficult the times were for our parents and everyone else, but we never had any feeling of neglect or hardship that I can remember.

We always had food on our table, and a comfortable place to live, so what else does a kid need? For me, I actually believe the Depression Era helped set me up for a life of thankfulness for the things that children from later years took for granted.

There are scenarios in my Memory Bank from the time I was two or three-years-old. Before you jump all over me with – "this guy is nuts! How can he remember things from way back then?" – concentrate on when you were that age. See, you do remember way back to early childhood!

My mother was Irish and grew up in Cambridge, Massachusetts. The staple for most Depression families was potatoes, and my mother must have gotten her genius for potato recipes from her Irish mother and father. Baked potatoes with creamed chip beef on top – mashed potatoes the same way – scalloped potatoes – any kind of potato hash – beef, chicken, plain vegetable, you name it – it made great hash. We lived on potatoes and vegetables, and I never had a bad meal. In later years in the Marine Corps eating c-rations in Korea, I never had a bad meal. I learned from the Depression!

My mother always had a pot of beef bones simmering on the stove. It not only always smelled good, but when that broth was turned into a Mulligan Stew, it was fit for a king. My father wasn't an all-around good cook, but he did love to make stew, as I do to this day.

If you've never had fish chowder loaded with codfish, onions, and potatoes, with a touch of salt pork for flavor, you haven't lived. A cheap meal in the Depression I guess, but six bucks for a small cup now with no fish in it!

All of us have hundreds of little tidbits in our Memory Bank that make us think of our parents. When I empty out our refrigerator into a pot on the stove and simmer it all day, I have vivid memories of my father. When I put creamed chipped beef on toast for breakfast I smile thinking of my mother.

They both carried us through the Depression, and we didn't even know there was one. *They* sure did, but they never let us know there was. That bit of magic will always be in a special spot in my Memory Bank. Dig around in yours – you'll know what I mean.

JAKE WIRTH'S

In 1868, the doors of Jake Wirth's Restaurant opened in Boston – and it's still going strong on Stuart St. and nothing much has changed. The wonderful aroma of bratwurst, sauerkraut, and many other German specialties hits you like a breath of fresh air…you're back home!

When I was a kid we lived on West Cedar St. in an apartment on Beacon Hill. My first trip to Jake's was around 1935, when I was four-years-old – could have been 1936, when I turned five though. I walked up Charles Street, crossed the Common, down Tremont Street, left on Stuart, and there you were – in heaven! My wonderful father, Harold Orth, would take me over to Jake's for lunch.

I remember to this day when he sat me up on the mahogany bar, and I had a sip of the stein of dark beer he was served. Then, at our table we had the amazing dark bread bratwurst sandwich with sauerkraut, and I was introduced to potato pancakes!

When I was older, my dad would take me to a Harvard football game at the stadium in Cambridge and then over to Jake's for an early dinner. How I loved it!

Flash ahead to 1971. I had been transferred back to good old Boston from New York by Fairchild Publications. Our small sales office was on the 5th floor at 7 Tremont Street. The view out the back window was of Jake's parking lot and the back entrance to heaven!

There were three other advertising sales guys there with other Fairchild publications, and at least once a week we'd walk out the back door, through the parking lot and into Jake's for lunch. We'd have a couple of bratwurst sandwiches, two or three darks, and toast each other for being 200 miles away from the home office in New York!

Every time I entered Jake's, I'd think of my time with my father, and when he was alive I'd take him to the great establishment as he did for me many years earlier.

There are some great eating and drinking spots in Boston, but for me, the top one is Jake Wirth's. I can close my eyes, and then visualize being there with my father. What a time we had!

BEANIE

In 1939, I was eight-years-old and my sister Julie was about three. For some reason I called her "Beanie" until she was around six. Then she told me to please call her Julie, as the name Beanie was for kids!

On Free Street, in Hingham where we lived, there were three or four boys my age that I played with all the time. Once in awhile my mother would say, "Jack, why don't you take Beanie with you for an hour or two?" Near our house was a dirt road down to a large sandpit alongside a beautiful pine grove. The guys loved going there, and today was no different even though they grumbled about Beanie tagging along. She had a ball, as we did, digging in the sand making a fort.

Then we sat in the pine grove to cool off, and David Rogers had a great idea. Out of his pocket came a small box of wooden matches. We put a few short twigs on a pile of pine needles and decided to have a small fire. Within minutes the breeze picked up and the flames spread to the surrounding pine needles, and we couldn't put out the fire!

We all ran at full speed, Beanie by my side being dragged along. When we reached home, my mother called the fire department, and the engines roared down Free Street. We had visions of the whole forest going up in smoke, but in a half-hour the firemen knocked on our door. I was petrified and ran into my room.

Within a couple of minutes my mother asked me to come out and talk to the fireman. I had this very real feeling that I would be going to reform school, and tears were about to roll down my cheeks.

The fireman asked who had lit the fire. I told him we all did except Beanie. "Where did you get the matches?" he asked. I told him I wasn't really sure who had them.

After a ten-minute lecture on fire safety, he said the other parents had also called the department, and he would visit them too. Then, he said something that would stick in my mind forever.

"You did the right thing in sticking up for your friends, and you're all responsible for the fire. Always remember that it may not have been you who lit the match, but you could have stopped it from happening. When you know you're doing something wrong always voice your opinion. You'll feel better about yourself."

From then on, whenever I would leave to play with the guys, Beanie would pipe up, "Don't bring any matches with you!"

My mother wrote the fire department a note, and strongly suggested I write a note to the fireman. I did, and carry on doing so to this day to anyone who lends me a helping hand like the fireman did!

AIN'T

When my sister, Ann, who I always called "Sister," and my younger sister, Julie, took our annual Christmas drive to Boston in the '40s to see the "Aunts," it was never a welcome visit for us. The Aunts and Uncle George weren't really aunts or uncle to us, but that's what we called them.

They lived in a beautiful old three or four-story townhouse on Bay State Road in Boston. We'd all dress in our Sunday best, and be told to be extremely polite and to smile a lot. This one Christmas, Sister was about ten, I was nine, and Julie around three. Julie was an adorable kid, and an absolute genius on the piano. Where Sister and I had failed at our efforts to become superstars, Julie had hit the jackpot!

When lunch was served, a maid served us (the children) in the kitchen. The meal never changed: carrot salad sandwiches with raisins, with the crust cut off the bread. Perhaps they thought we were friendly with Bugs Bunny or Mr. and Mrs. Rabbit! Nevertheless, Sister told the maid, the Aunts, and Uncle George that the lunch was wonderful, and we followed suit, as we were allowed to sit in the beautiful living room with the grownups.

A month or so before the visit to Bay State Road, Julie somehow had heard someone use the word "ain't" in a sentence. My mother, in her own calm way, explained to Julie that "ain't" was not a nice word to use and to please not use it again. My father seconded the motion, and added that it could be considered a naughty word.

Well, there sat the grand piano in the living room – a Steinway, of course. My mother had told the Aunts and Uncle George about Julie's amazing progress on the piano and they asked her if she'd like to play for them.

Julie said, "No, thank you!"

My mother, we knew, was steaming, but very calmly asked Julie to play a short piece, and began to lead Julie over to the Steinway.

Suddenly Julie stopped in her tracks as she turned and screamed, "Ain't! Ain't! Ain't! Ain't!"

My mother couldn't help herself, or hold back the laughter, and my father joined her. Julie didn't play the piano, and Sister and I had a newly found respect for Julie!

When I took that story out of my Memory Bank, the first thing I thought of was that it was a good thing that episode came about in 1941 or so. For, if you did a fast forward to today, the Aunts and Uncle George would have heard a much stronger swear word than "Ain't!"

THE SEARS ROEBUCK CATALOG

Back in the 1920s, '30s, and '40s, and I guess long before that, practically every family had a Sears Roebuck Catalog! As I remember in the '30s, it was as thick as a New York phone book, and had everything known to man or woman in it. There was nothing you couldn't buy from a Sear's catalog, and I loved to look at every page, even before I could read!

My mother and father would both read stories to us. We had a few of the nursery rhymes memorized, and could probably recite "The Three Little Pigs" without missing a beat, but my favorite book was the Sears Catalog. It must have been around 1938 that I started cutting items out of the catalog and keeping them in my room.

Our neighbor in Hingham worked for Sears Roebuck, and kept me supplied with my very own catalog. My dream of being a dairy farmer was brought to life by the catalog. I cut out all the work clothes I would need: overalls, boots, and jackets. Then, I had my farm equipment section: shovels, rakes, pitchforks, feed buckets, etc. I should have gone to work for Sears Roebuck in later years because I had the catalog memorized!

In a round about way, the catalog put me on the seat of a brand new bike, without it even being a birthday or Christmas gift! One of the great things in those days for a kid to keep things in was a cigar box, and my friend next door, who was the Sears Man, smoked cigars. When the box was gone, he'd present it to me to stack up in my room! I had boxes for all my Sears' products!

Each box was special, but the one that really stood out, and sat in a place of honor in my room, was one that I pasted a large photo of a bright red bike on the cover. I think the bike was called a Hi-Flyer, but I'm not sure of that. After all, it was seventy-two years ago!

Over the weeks and months, my mother would probably see that box in my room every day or so. Most of the comments about my Sears collection were about me owning my own dairy farm, and supplying milk to everyone in Hingham!

Spring finally arrived and we had a big plot in the back yard where our vegetable garden was. It was time to turn the soil over and get going with the planting. There was an old chicken coop near the garden that my father had cleaned up and we used it to store tools. My sister and I also played in there sometimes.

It must have been a Saturday, because both our mother and father were at home, and after breakfast we all went out to survey the garden area together. We were sent into the chicken coop to get our rakes and shovels, and stood in complete shock when we saw a bright red boy's bike and a bright blue girl's bike sitting there!

The sheer joy of a total surprise for a kid is one of the delights of life. My sister, Ann, and I could well have been the poster kids for a painting by Norman Rockwell on the cover of *The Saturday Evening Post* entitled "Pure Joy"! The Depression was still the topic of conversation those days, and I don't know how our parents worked it out to get those bikes.

For a number of days that red bike came in the house at night, and had a place of honor in my room! It was a long time before it ever saw the inside of the chicken coop again. It came in each night to be dusted off and put to sleep next to me!

I can't remember any gift giving me more pleasure than that wonderful bike, and just maybe that cigar box with the red bike on the cover had something to do with it! Thank you Sears Roebuck! Thank you Mom and Dad, and thanks to my Sears Roebuck neighbor!

CHRISTMAS ON FREE STREET

In 1938, the Depression wasn't far behind us, but I don't recall us ever giving it much thought. However, Sister and I somehow knew that our family wasn't laughing all the way to the bank. There were a lot of our neighbors on Free Street in Hingham that had kind of lost their way to the local financial institution, too!

Our parents always seemed to supply us with whatever we needed, and then some, and each Christmas we somehow received surprises we never counted on ever seeing under the tree. However, this Christmas might leave us all with a touch of the feelings we had after the terrible hurricane had passed through a couple of months before. Shock, sadness, and devastation don't mix with the Yuletide season, but let's just say Sister and I thought Santa would pass over our house on Free Street just as fast as those hurricane winds did.

Sister, in her own understanding way and in a roundabout approach, let me know gently that the electric train I wanted so badly would probably not reach the Free Street station. She also mentioned in passing that the doll she wanted for her collection would have to wait until next year to move in with her. She never made a big deal out of things like that, and if Sister didn't, I didn't, because after all, she was my big sister and always knew best.

"Jackie! Jackie! Come on, let's look under the tree!" Sister was up even before I was, and escorted me to the Christmas tree.

Not only had the train stopped at the station, it pulled up to a water tower, and was waiting patiently for the engineer! As I beamed with glee, I also noticed that the doll, Tina, had moved in, and even had a small suitcase with her. It was loaded with a wardrobe that would make Bette Davis envious!

15

I stopped the train just long enough to have our pancakes for breakfast, and Tina sat in Sister's lap at the kitchen table. I think both Sister and I knew for sure that Mom and Dad had found their way to the bank on December 24, 1938, and the teller laughed all the way to the vault as he escorted them in!

THE TOBOGGAN CHUTE

Whenever a family moves from one town to another, it seems like the weight of the world is suddenly placed on the young shoulders of the kids involved.

Will I ever see Pecky Honstra again? Will Sister ever see Pecky's sister, Audrey, again? How about Julie---will she ever see Mrs. Edwards again, the lady next door who would make her chocolate cakes and never let a day go by without seeing her? What about the toboggan---will there ever be a hill in Newton Center that was made for toboggans like the one in Hingham?

What a hill! To us, Triphammer Hill could just as well have been Mount Washington. It was huge, and the perfect spot for our toboggan to fly the three of us through the crisp winter air over its snowy crust at Olympian bobsled speeds! Sister was fearless as our leader, and always sat in the front taking the brunt of the wind, and used her uncanny knack of steering, which is no easy trick on a toboggan. Then, after each speed run down the slope, she'd let Julie stay on board and haul her back up the hill.

On the real steep part, she'd just utter two words, "Okay! Jackie!" I'd grab the towrope with her and help haul our cargo to the top of our mountain.

Would winter ever be the same without that snowy peak in Hingham?

Well, on our first full day in Newton Center, Sister and I walked down Pleasant Street a couple of hundred yards and turned right on Tyler Terrace. A few hundred yards down on the left, we looked out on the expanse of the Newton Center Playground. From the hill overlooking the beautiful property, you could see a stream running through the immaculate grounds, but what really caught our eye was the tower that sat on top of the hill. There was a wide, slanted ramp that went up twenty-five or thirty feet to a platform that overlooked the whole playground. The man painting the platform seemed overjoyed to explain what the tower was all about.

In his wonderful Italian accent, Tony DeStefano, the full time caretaker of the playground, told us about the toboggan chute. He explained, in detail, how they attached sections of a long chute to the tower in the late fall. Then, with the first heavy snow, Tony would pack the snow in the chutes down and spray them with water. In a few hours the chutes were icy runways just waiting to send tobogganers speeding down the hill and across the playground. Well, Sister and I couldn't wait to tell Julie, and Mom and Dad. If Triphammer Hill was Mount Washington, our newfound toboggan chute was Mount Everest!

Winter finally came! The night was as crisp and clear as it possibly could be as the spotlights on the tower flashed through the snowflakes, turning them into diamonds as they flitted in front of us. Tony, making sure each passenger was tucked in safely, pushed each toboggan off the platform down the icy passageway!

Sister, of course, was our leader as usual, and I never heard her yell with so much excitement. Well, maybe on the roller coaster at Paragon Park, but certainly at no other time! Julie sat between us, and wasn't quite sure if she liked her first trip on the chute, but three rides later she was screaming with joy like hundreds of others were.

Mom made us hot chocolate, and between sips, we couldn't stop relaying our exciting speed runs to her and Dad. We were only thirty-five miles or so away from Hingham, but we could just as well be in Lake Placid, New York at the Winter Olympics as far as we were concerned. Sister, once again, was right. When we moved she told Julie and me that we had exciting things to look forward to in Newton Center. The playground turned into just one of the many wonderful things in store for us.

In later years when visiting Hingham, our Mount Washington wasn't a mountain anymore…just a small hill, and the toboggan chute really didn't carry Sister, Julie, and me at breakneck speeds across the snowy baseball diamond of the playground. I miss those days of being a kid, when everything seemed bigger, faster, more exciting than they truly were.

But you know, as far as I'm concerned, when Sister, Julie, and I would crush ourselves together and fly down that chute, we went at least 100 miles an hour! I can still hear the sounds of the toboggan gliding over the ice, and Sister telling us we'd take two more speed runs and go home for some hot chocolate.

Wonderful days with my two sisters!

THE BUGLE BOY

When a nine-year-old boy, soon to be ten, moves with his family from Hingham to Newton Center, just outside of Boston, Massachusetts, in the summer of 1941, the weight of the world seemed to be on his shoulders! He didn't know anyone, and his older sister, Ann, only eleven but with the capabilities of a doctorate in philosophy, stated, "You'll find a lifelong friend within days, Jackie, so just relax!"

Well, "Sister," as the kid always called Ann, had never been wrong in his few years of enjoying life, so why should it be any different now? Within twenty-four hours the sound of a bugle would announce the new friend's entrance into the life of the new kid on the block.

The sound of the horn didn't come anywhere near imitating a possible Harry James in the neighborhood, as the loud blasts sounded like the cavalry bugler galloping full speed in retreat, trying desperately to signal the troops to follow him! However, like a call-to-arms, it brought Jackie out of the house in a flash and over to a short fence behind the garage, where the semi-musical blasts came from.

There, in the next yard, was a kid running around a pine tree with an older gentleman chasing him, without any possibility of catching him. At twenty second intervals the boy would stop, give the old man a blast from the bugle, laugh hysterically, continue his jaunt around the yard next to the old man's, and disappear through the lilac bushes.

Jack immediately knew that Bugle Boy was his kind of kid, and set out down Pleasant Street to find the "wannabe" musician with the beat up horn. The big gray house, the third one down from his, would become his home away from home for the next few years, and his association with Dave would be one of the great events in his life.

They would remain friends for life, and in their mid-seventies would realize more than ever, that if that kid with the golden horn hadn't decided to rattle Mr. Powell's cage, they may never have met! Well, they would have met under different circumstances, but it wouldn't have been quite the same.

The sound of the bugle, and the whole scene, set the stage. It meant that the kid with the horn had a great imagination, perhaps directed in the wrong direction that day for some, but not for Jack. To him, it meant, "Life was just a bowl of cherries" for Bugle Boy, and picking cherries from the tree of life with that kid would never be dull... and it never was!

How fortunate they were, and are, to have literally hundreds of wonderful memories of those days in Newton Center together. You're only a kid for a few years, and you should never let time go by without filling your Memory Bank with happenings of your youth. We, Dave and Jack, went to the The Bank often, and deposited a long list of memorable stories. With long-term interest, those memories are now worth a fortune! In fact, as the Master Card promotion states, "They're priceless!"

Thanks, Dave, for blowing that horn those many years ago. I can still hear the notes, and Harry James, and the other greats that followed, never created what you did with their music. *You* opened our account at The Memory Bank...and...oh, how sweet it is!

THE KID ON TARLETON ROAD

The bus ride from Derry, New Hampshire to Boston, Massachusetts only took a couple of hours. I took that route at least once a month while attending Pinkerton Academy in Derry during the mid-1940s.

By the time I reached my house in Newton Center, the sun had gone down and a beautiful, late fall evening welcomed me, as did my family, for a weekend at home. After dinner and updating my family on life at Pinkerton, I ran down Pleasant Street at full speed to Tarleton Road to, hopefully, see my great friend, Don Duncklee.

"Dunk" was a kid my own age with the daring of a Houdini within him that he would release on a fairly regular basis, to the delight of his close friends! I happened to be one of the chosen few to hold membership in that group, and would be forever proud to renew that annual membership well past the year 2010!

On this one fall evening, I peered up at the well-lit window on the third floor of the old New England Duncklee home. By bouncing a pebble or two off the window, it was easy to arouse the curiosity of Dunk, who opened the window, and without hesitation went into his "exit through the window" mode! Just as the acrobat was hanging from the windowsill preparing to drop down to the porch roof, the front screen porch door opened, and Mr. Duncklee appeared on the porch!

I hid behind a tree across the street as Mr. "D" relaxed while taking in the fall air. His second oldest son, Donnie, hung noiselessly from the upstairs window. In touch-and-go situations like this one, seconds seem to turn into long minutes, and minutes turn into eternity! Well, time ran out on the high-flying acrobat, and in an effort to climb back into his room, Dunk's feet hit the side of the house with a loud "bang"!

Mr. Duncklee, in a very calm, but loud voice, pierced the air with, "Donald, is that you? Get down from there!"

Well, Dunk let go, landed with a crash on the porch roof, climbed down to the porch below, and faced his father. I was behind the tree, and could barely hold my laughter as Donnie was escorted back into his house by the senior Duncklee! I'm sure Mr. "D" knew that somewhere, outside lurking in the shadows, was one of Donnie's many admirers.

Perhaps that's one of the reasons why Mr. Duncklee was known to exaggerate on Donnie's whereabouts when I would call on the phone. A typical conversation could be: "Hello, Mr. Duncklee. Is Don there, please?"

"No, Jack. He's in Oklahoma!" Or…"No, Jack. He's in Utah, and why aren't you at the library?!"

Those phone calls always brought a smile to my face, for I knew Dunk would appear shortly at the playground or at Jolly Hollow or en route to Bobby Gregory's house on Commonwealth Avenue. Then, Jimmie Emmert, Dickie Farr, Billy Fortune, David Clough, Teddy Ripley, and a few others would join forces and have a great time playing *Mumbly-peg*, *Rolly at the Bat*, or sneak a cigarette in some safe hideaway!

Life was good in those 1940s!

THE P-38 FIGHTER PLANE

During WWII many young boys were really into putting together airplane models of the planes used during the war. I never had the patience to do many, but I'll never forget the P-38 I "borrowed" from the Five and Ten in Newton Center Square in 1941 or '42!

It was a great summer day, and David Clough and I walked the half mile or so up to the Square to get a pineapple sherbet cone at Morgan Brother's Creamery. The summer deal was four cents for a huge scoop of sherbet, and to this day I think of that happening every time I open a container of Publix Pineapple Sherbet! I had four cents and forked it over to Morgan's gladly, and headed to the Five and Ten with David where he wanted to get an airplane model. I would only be an onlooker, for my pockets had been drained of my life savings – four cents!

This was one of those great Five and Tens that had the soda fountain/sandwich bar, and they made great vanilla and cherry cokes! But with no cash I ignored the fountain area, and went to the back of the store with David. What a selection they had. Planes of every vintage, and most were only ten cents which included the directions, all the balsa wood parts, decals, airplane glue, etc.

While Dave was picking out his plane, I spotted the P-38. Like a bolt of lightening out of nowhere, which penetrated my small brain saying, "Take that model," I became a shoplifter! I put the P-38 under my shirt and walked out of the Five and Ten. I'm sure it was my first experience, at ten years old, to steal something, and I know walking home I had a strange feeling about it. But not strange enough to return the stolen goods!

Later that day my mother saw me laying out the model parts on a table in the sun porch and asked where I got it. When I told her the Five and Ten, with what I'm sure was a sheepish look, she asked where I had gotten the money. There was no sense to even try to lie to my mother. She could read me like a book, especially when I was only ten years old.

With tears in my eyes I told her I had stolen it. Well, there was no screaming and yelling. Somehow I wished there were. For my mother to calmly tell me she was heart broken and disappointed in me was far worse than any loud outburst.

Within five minutes we were walking down Pelham Street toward the Square and the dreaded return to the Five and Ten with the wonderful P-38. My job was to tell the manager what I had done, and give back the model along with an apology. My mother offered to pay for the returned model that had been opened, but the manager said that wasn't necessary. Then he looked me in the eye and said something like this, which I've never forgotten.

"You're a very lucky young man to have a mother who cares for you so much. You know you shouldn't have taken that model, and your mother wants you to know that no matter how much you want something, the only way to get it is the honest way. Whenever you're in this store and see a model you want and have no money, you and I can make arrangements for you to have it. You can pay me weekly until the ten cents is covered!"

I never took him up on his offer but continued to go into his store. One time he actually saw me and asked how my mother was. I'm sure he was as impressed with her as I was!

THE KID BEHIND THE FENCE

In the summer of, let's say 1943, my mother sent me up to Newton Center Square to get a haircut. Hmmm...sure wish I had hair today at the age of seventy-nine, but that's another story!

If you had thirty-four cents in your pocket, you could get your hair cut at Mr. Anthony's, then walk next door to Garb's Drug Store, and get a vanilla coke from Arthur at the marble counter. You would then cross the street to Morgan Brother's Creamery, and get a pineapple sherbet ice cream cone. All of this for thirty-four cents!!!

My mother would usually only give me a quarter, and I'd spring for the extra nine cents if I had it. Then, I'd walk down Pelham Street with my pineapple gem, turn right to go down the hill to 112 Pleasant Street. Home again at last!

This one particular day was different. At the end of Pelham Street before hitting the home stretch for our house, there was a kid behind the fence in the yard on the left. He had just moved in, as I had never seen him before. A "Hi" was in order, and the "Hi" in return turned into a sixty-seven-year friendship that is still going strong as we enter 2011!

There was something about this kid behind the fence that turned his "Hi" answering my "Hi" into an imaginary greeting of "I'm Jimmy, and I just moved here. Sure glad you came along today, as I'm sick of staring at this fence all by myself, wondering how I'll survive in this corral of loneliness."

OK, so I'm a little dramatic, but you know what I mean. To say a twelve-year-old kid took a ten-and-a-half-year-old kid under his wing may be an exaggeration, but I'm telling ya, a couple of months later we became two birds of a feather!

Time flew by. We had a clubhouse called The Coop in my garage. There we snuck cigarettes, played cards, had a few beers long before the age of twenty-one, and looked out for each other over the years.

Jimmy was my first driving school attendee. I, of course, had no license, but did have the use of my father's car for midnight rides. Paul Revere had his horse for his midnight ride. We had my father's '37 Ford "woodie" wagon called a beach wagon in New England back then. Jimmy, after driving over a few lawns and crossing a yellow line or two, graduated with honors. Then, he had a few years left before he could get his official license, but I gave him a temporary one!

The years passed by. We graduated from Newton High School in the class of 1950. Jim went to General Motors Institute in Michigan. I joined the United States Marine Corps. I shall never forget a phone call I received in September of 1953 from Jim. I was in the Yokosoka Naval Hospital in Japan. The Korean War was over, but I had been wounded for the third time a week before the war ended in July, and sent by hospital ship to Japan.

I was called to the nurse's office, and had a person-to-person call from Newton, Massachusetts from Jimmy! I don't know how many quarters he had to put in the pay phone, but I could hear the coins dropping into the cash box. That phone call kind of summed up our friendship... we took care of each other!

Jimmy is still The Kid behind the Fence to me! We're brothers, even to the point of having a tattoo on our left shoulder that no one knew about for many months. Our wonderful friend, Bobby, had the same one. But that's a story for another day. If ya ever see a kid behind a fence say, "Hi," and I hope you're as lucky as I was on that day in 1943!

LSMFT

Some genius ad person came up with this slogan for Lucky Strike Cigarettes in the 1940s: "Lucky Strike Means Fine Tobacco." Back in those days a huge percentage of people smoked, and very little thought, if any, was given to the possibility that smoking wasn't good for you. In fact, my mother in later years told us her doctor suggested she smoke cigarettes to calm her down during her pregnancy in 1930 when my sister, Ann, was born!

For kids to smoke was a different story. We were told at an early age that smoking would stunt our growth, so wait until you're fully grown to light up. That always reminds me of the story of Little Johnny who was told never to masturbate for it would cause blindness. Little Johnny thought about that and said, "Mommy, can't I just do it until I have to wear glasses?"

When WWII began in 1941, it became difficult to buy name brand cigarettes. Lucky Strike advertised the fact that they had "gone to war," and the bulk of their smokes were sent to servicemen. Off-brand cigarettes came on the market: Fatimas, Wings, Raleighs, etc. That was the era my friends and I started sneaking cigarettes whenever we had a chance. The first puff I ever took was on a Fatima when I was about twelve-years-old.

One of my favorite pastimes was smoking tea, dried corn silk, and even crushed pine needles! You wanna get a real jolt? Inhale a pipe full of pine needles! The pipe was great because two or three kids could sit in the pine grove and take drags on the pipe like Indians with the peace pipe. If you were lucky enough to be able to confiscate a quart of Pickwick Ale, also known as poor man's whiskey, it made for an even better time!

My sister, Ann, caught me smoking the pipe and I told her it was only tea I was smoking. In my room I kept a small tin on my bookshelf with a pack of Fatimas in it for special occasions. I opened the box one day to find a little note inside that said, "This isn't tea, Jackie!" She never told our mother or father though!

You could buy smokes from a cigarette machine – put in a quarter and get three cents back which was tucked into cellophane on the side of the pack. If you could buy cigarettes in the store they were around seventeen cents a pack, so we smoked more tea than real tobacco.

We thought we were men-of-the-world putting something over on our parents. We had arrived. We smoked. We had a beer here and there. It was heaven to grow up in the 1940s.

DECEMBER 7, 1941

President Franklin Delano Roosevelt's message to Congress on December 8, 1941, to declare war on Japan and Germany: "Yesterday, December 7, 1941, is a date which will live in infamy. The United States of America was suddenly and deliberately attacked by naval and air forces of the Empire of Japan."

It was a Sunday. Every Sunday we had a wonderful family dinner at one o'clock. My younger sister, Julie, was four-years-old. My older sister, by a year and a couple of months, Ann, who was always "Sister" to me, was eleven. In three days, December 10, I would be ten-years-old.

Dinner on that Sunday didn't have the usual flair, the usual enthusiasm for a roast chicken dinner, pot roast, roast beef, or whatever our mother served. The Japanese had struck Pearl Harbor. The casualties and damage were huge, and war had been declared on both Japan and Germany.

Our parents and millions of others had battled their way through the Great Depression over the past ten years, and things had just started looking up in the late 1930s. The next four years would bring rationing of food and gasoline, and a war effort by military and civilians alike that would bring victory in 1945. Then, the returning veterans and their generation would expand our country in leaps and bounds. Yet, five years later we were involved in another war, in Korea, then Vietnam, then the Gulf War, then Iraq, and time will tell if and when the world continues once again on a destructive path.

After dinner on that December day, I ran to my good friend David Clough's house, three doors down on Pleasant Street. The same anger, gloom, and sadness filled his house, as it did all over America. We went up to Dave's third floor bedroom, where you could look across to one end of the beautiful Newton Center playground. Even the playground had lost its luster on that day, as if it had joined the President in announcing the changing of our lives.

Dave got out his huge collection of lead soldiers, trucks, and tanks, and we prepared them for battle. Then, on the other side of the room, we set up another platoon of troops. These were the Japanese forces, as we, in our own way, had declared war, too. The final commitment was as decisive and quick as the attack on Pearl Harbor. Dave cut a small Japanese flag out of the world atlas, and we glued it to a matchstick and attached it to the Japanese tank. The same was done with the American flag for our valiant soldiers on that Sunday afternoon.

The battle on the third floor in the wonderful gray house on Pleasant Street was over quickly, and we avenged Pearl Harbor right then and there. Little did we know that in nine years Dave would wear the uniform of the U.S. Air Force, and I would wear the uniform of the U.S. Marine Corps because in June of 1950, the Korean War began.

That Sunday in 1941 is as clear in my mind as last Sunday was. The news on that day was no bed of roses either. Our country is in turmoil over many issues, and the terrible war in Iraq gets worse with time. None of us can release the frustration and sadness by cutting a flag out of an atlas, as we did in 1941. We're in our mid-seventies now, and snipping the colors from a book doesn't work anymore. But sixty-five years ago for a couple of ten-year-old boys, it seemed like the right thing to do.

THE VICTORY GARDENS

In Mayport, Florida, William, the tomato guy, parks his pickup near the water every weekend and sells wonderful tomatoes, watermelons, cantaloupes, and corn. He drives down to Plant City every Thursday, and loads up with the freshest stuff you've ever eaten! I'm a weekly customer, and enjoy talking to William almost as much as I enjoy eating his produce!

Last Saturday afternoon I sat down by the little pond we live on, and husked a dozen ears of corn, courtesy of William. It was flashback time for me, and The Bank was open for business, even though it was a Saturday. It was 1942, and I was at our house in Newton Center, Massachusetts. I was shucking corn from our Victory Garden, which was about six or seven hundred yards down Pleasant Street at the Newton Center Playground.

World War II was in full swing in both the Pacific area with Japan, and in Europe with Germany. Young American men and women by the millions were in the military, working in defense plants, steel mills, ammunition depots, etc. Gasoline, food, clothing…you name it…was hard to come by, and most items were rationed. Everything was directed to the war effort, and farmers of America were doing their best to supply all of us with food.

However, there were shortages of everything. With incredible speed and much enthusiasm, Victory Gardens sprang up in towns all over America in the spring of 1942. Empty lots, areas at parks, playgrounds, golf courses, campgrounds, etc. were hoed and harrowed, and Mr. and Mrs. America and their kids became farmers!

The Newton Center Playground, one of the great recreational gems ever, set aside a large area for the gardens, and my father was one of the first to sign up for a garden plot. No fees… no real estate tax… just a shake of hands between Tony DeStefano, the wonderful superintendent of the playground, and my father. Just a gentleman's agreement, if you will, that each gardener would care for the land as if it were their own, and let Mother Nature do the rest!

Each garden was about 30 feet x 30 feet as I remember, and in late May or early June, my father proceeded to turn me into a laborer on our little farm! My sister, Ann, and I, my sister Julie was too young, were recruited to help with the planting, weeding, and eventually, the picking of the vegetables. We complained, as kids will do, but there was something I really loved about the whole deal!

The Victory Garden was sort of a school away from school for me for three or four summers. In fact, I firmly believe I learned more at the "little farm" than I ever did at school! There was no sprinkler system and no running water, but there was a small brook nearby, and I know I lugged thousands of pails of water to our patch of greenery. If you wanted something to turn out well, you had to sweat a little (or a lot!) to make it happen. Somehow, I never learned that in school, but I sure did at the Victory Garden!

I also learned a lot about people from time spent at the garden. Most of the thirty or forty gardening families were friendly, and enjoyed trying to grow bigger and better vegetables than the farmer in the next plot. But...even those people were quick to join together and condemn someone who traveled a somewhat different path.

Mr. and Miss Frost, brother and sister, were our neighbors on Pleasant Street. They were much older than my parents, but weren't yet retired. Mr. Frost was an old-time bookkeeper with the United Fruit Company in Boston. He would trudge to the train each workday wearing the same old suit and overcoat, and carrying a large, well-worn leather briefcase. Miss Frost would always wear old, long dresses, as she, too, walked a little different route to Newton Center to catch the bus for Newton Corner. She was a librarian at the branch library there.

They lived in an old Victorian house next to us, but the house was completely surrounded by trees and undergrowth, which made it invisible from the street and almost so from our yard. The Frosts had a huge barn/garage at the bottom of their property on Pleasant Street. This was equipped with electricity, but we were never sure that their house was. The only lights we ever saw within the house were of kerosene lanterns, which caused a dull, spooky kind of light to move by a window. They lived the life of hermits, when not heading off to work, and stayed completely to themselves.

There were numerous people at the playground the day the Victory Garden plots were handed out. To everyone's surprise, the Frosts were there, and dressed ready to go to work. If you didn't know better, you'd swear the year was 1842, not 1942! They were clad in work outfits similar to those seen in old photos of coal miners leaving the mines after a twelve-hour day of torturous work!

There were whispers ranging from – "What are the Frosts doing here?" to "I don't think they deserve a Victory Garden!" Well, they got one… and it was right next to ours!

My father, in his own calm way, which in later life I admired a great deal, taught me a lesson that has remained with me until this day. On many an occasion he called me "Jackson," and that day at the playground he instilled a philosophy in me that I've always been grateful for.

"Jackson, always remember you can't judge a book by its cover. You've got to open the book and your mind, and not jump to conclusions about anything. Mr. and Miss Frost may be a little different from some and travel a different route through life. You and I will be spending a lot of time at the Victory Garden, and with the Frosts since their plot is next to ours. Let's help them out if we can, and become their friends. Everyone needs to see a smiling face now and then, so let's enjoy our planting with the Frosts."

Out of the Frost's barn came every tool needed to cultivate a garden. They each had a wheelbarrow, the kind with removable wooden slats on each side. Every Saturday morning they'd head for the garden loaded down with moist, rich, compost from their compost pit in their tree-laden yard. Their garden became the "garden of gardens," and every garden on the playground was dwarfed by theirs.

They planted corn around the perimeter of the garden, and in no time they had a six-foot fence of corn stalks. Within the "fence" grew the finest tomatoes, squash, spinach, carrots, etc., that anyone had ever seen. Talk about organic gardening… they were masters at it!

One Saturday I asked Miss Frost if she wanted some help pushing the wheelbarrow, which was loaded down with compost, down to the garden. With a look of pleasant surprise she accepted, and Mr. Frost and I went side-by-side down Pleasant Street with our wheelbarrows, with Miss Frost behind us. I had also put a flat of tomato plants on top of the compost, as I was going to plant them that day.

I had just finished digging a couple of holes for the tomatoes, when Mr. Frost appeared with a bucket of compost and suggested that I put some in each hole. I did, and it was the beginning of an education for me. Here I was, an eleven-year-old kid who wasn't going to judge a book by it's cover, and I'm sure glad I didn't. The following Saturday was the same scenario as we headed for the gardens real early with the wheelbarrows loaded down, but a couple of hours later something wonderful happened.

Mr. and Miss Frost asked me to come over to their garden. Attached to Mr. Frost's overalls was a thin chain dangling down into a pocket. When he pulled the chain out of the pocket, there was a leather pouch attached to it. The pouch had a tiny padlock on it that he opened, and he took out two quarters.

"We want to pay you for helping us, Jack, and would like to do so each week if you'd like to continue working with us."

Well, I hadn't really expected any money! I told them I was happy to help them when I could, but didn't expect to be paid.

Miss Frost, who very seldom said a word to anyone, said to me in an extremely soothing voice, "Jack, your helping us is very generous of you, and such a pleasant experience for Mr. Frost and me. Please allow us to give you a small amount each week in appreciation of your company and work efforts."

Well, first of all, two quarters...fifty cents...wasn't a small amount of money in 1941, especially for a kid! But more than that, I knew from their manner that they truly wanted me to accept their money and their friendship. Another thing I learned that day...I learned that there are some times that you would hurt someone's feelings if you didn't allow them to reciprocate with a kindness of their own.

We made an unspoken deal at the Victory Garden that day. I was happy as could be on many occasions when Mr. Frost would open the leather pouch, and produce quarters for me, and I knew they were just as happy as I was!

Over the years the Frosts gave me, and my sisters, Ann and Julie, wonderful boxes of Hilliard's candy on just about every holiday, and we knew they enjoyed doing it. We, in turn, enjoyed helping the Frosts out now and then with little chores, and for two or three summers, I continued to learn from the Frosts. My father and I had the second best Victory Garden on the playground! Second only to the Frosts, whose garden was actually a jungle of the healthiest plantings you've ever seen.

In the mid-1800s, Henry David Thoreau wrote: "If a man does not keep pace with his companions, perhaps it is because he hears a different drummer. Let him step to the music which he hears, however measured or far away."

The Frosts *did* march to a different drummer, but I was fortunate enough to learn at the Victory Garden not to judge a book by its cover, and that dancing or marching to a different tune is just another option people can enjoy.

Until 1950, when I graduated from Newton High School, I continued to lend a hand to the Frosts. They remained in their hermit-like existence, only venturing out to either work or the Victory Garden. They had no transportation, and all of their subsistence requirements came from their Garden of Eden at the playground. Miss Frost canned hundreds of jars of vegetables, and they literally lived off the land to the point where Mr. Frost would bring a small jar of swiss chard to work each day for lunch.

In November of 1950, I left Newton Center for three years of duty with the United States Marine Corps. The Korean War had begun in June of that year. In 1953, while I was in Korea, my parents moved to an apartment in Newton Highlands. Until that time, the Frosts would continually inquire into how I was doing.

In thinking back, I've always had a feeling that the Victory Gardens played a huge part in bringing much happiness to the Frosts, and in many ways, those gardens did the same for me. The gardens, my father, and the Frosts showed me that to judge a book by its cover is a major mistake.

In my book of life, I've met a lot of interesting people in all walks of life. The chapter including the Frosts and the Victory Gardens is one of my favorites!

AN OASIS IN NEWTON CENTER

It wasn't just a playground…it was an oasis that supplied us with a way of life that will never be seen again. There it sat…ten miles, as the crow flies, from Fenway Park in Boston. The crowds at Fenway, even for a Ted Williams blast into the bullpen in right field, couldn't have been more enthusiastic than the lucky ones who made the Brewer Playground in Newton Center their home away from home.

From my bedroom on Pleasant Street, an appropriate name for any byway near the playground, I could gaze through the trees and see the Victory Gardens at one end of the complex. A few acres had been set aside for local residents to grow vegetables during World War II. From 1942 to 1946, my father, sisters, and I planted and picked bushels of the best produce our mother ever set before us. A Sunday dinner that included Golden Bantam corn, Kentucky Wonder beans, tomatoes, and summer squash that was picked less than an hour before you devoured it made the garden chores well worthwhile.

Food rationing was in full force in support of all the military branches, and Victory gardens were located in most of the villages in Newton. On a warm summer day, with the marvelous crack of the bat sound echoing toward the tomatoes, I could work faster than any farmer could in New England. Then, head for the diamond thinking I was only a couple years away from joining the lineup at Fenway with the Sox!

After a few hours of chasing fly balls and imitating our national pastime heroes, most of whom had left the game behind to serve their country, it was back to the small patch of vegetation that seemed to continuously beg for water. A narrow stream meandered through the center of our Shangri-La, and with buckets in hand, I made dozens of trips to the brook to insure that meals would always include well-watered treats.

Within home run distance of the gardens, on the grounds of the great oasis, lived Tony DeStefano and his family. We never gave it much thought then, but now, sixty years later, I wonder how many playgrounds in the United States had a full-time caretaker that lived right on the grounds. Tony worked for the City of Newton, and treated the Brewer landscape as if it was his own private estate. He manicured the entire area constantly, and we were guests allowed to roam around as long as we, too, treated the cherished property like the gem it was.

From behind the cornstalks that surrounded many of the gardens, you could hear the clucking of Tony's chickens. Closing your eyes for a moment, you'd swear you were on a farm in New Hampshire, not ten miles away from the finish of the Boston Marathon. The chickens supplied a select group of DeStefano customers with the best eggs east of the Mississippi. Well, at least east of the Charles River!

Of course, I loved the eggs, but better still, it gave me the chance to see Eleanor, Tony's daughter, when I picked up our allotment of hen delights. You'd have thought I had one of those eggs in my mouth, as I always seemed to stammer when it came time to talk to Eleanor. I don't think I got over that when talking to girls until I was at least sixteen!

On any given Saturday during the summer and fall, you'd hear the whistle of hundreds of arrows piercing the air and thumping into straw targets set up not far from the gardens. Archery experts from all over New England would compete in tournaments on the amazing property where a few hundred years before Indian arrows flew toward a target that supplied food and clothing for tribes of the area. The archers set up luncheon spreads that would make the Ritz at the Public Gardens proud, and serve cocktails in glassware to rival Locke Ober's, the great Boston eatery.

On following weekends, the cast of characters, and the sport would change drastically. The wonderfully accented Bahamian cricket team, dressed in perfectly ironed white trousers with shirts to match, shook hands with the British team…and the game was on. We, of the baseball mind, didn't understand the game, but loved the athletic grace with which the "bowler" would wind up and let the ball go toward the batter. It seemed as though he would stay at the plate, called the wicket, for hours on end with a cricket bat in hand. Hundreds of people, with accents not learned in Boston, watched the cricket matches. They too, enjoyed an array of luncheon specialties, but none quite on the scale of gourmet bow and arrow enthusiasts.

The cricket players, in their beanie-like, small visored caps, and their array of followers, spelled profit for me. I'd pull my red wagon over to the Jenney gas station that bordered the other end of the great oasis, and load up with Coca-Cola. Coke sold for five cents, plus a two-cent deposit on the bottle. For ten cents a bottle, I could barely keep up with the demand, and after returning the bottles, I had a five-cent profit on each drink.

Those nickels eventually added up to enough dollars to purchase a Rawlings claw Ferris Fain first baseman's mitt that was supposed to be my ticket to stardom with the Sox! Sure wish I still had that glove, even though the only part of Fenway Park it ever saw was the bleachers as I sat, glove in hand, hoping for the chance to field a home run ball as it cleared the 420 foot mark on the center field wall.

Each playground in the Newton's had a traveling baseball team of twelve and thirteen-year-old kids. West

Newton, Newton Highlands, Waban, Newton Upper Falls, etc. all fielded teams. The only adult involved was Buck, the man in charge of recreation for the city. Buck made sure each team was supplied with a new game ball each week, and he'd record all the game scores. On game days we'd hop on our bikes and head out together without a care in the world. What wonderful days those were!

Bobby Gregory, our own left-handed answer to Warren Spahn of the Boston Braves, pitched us to many a victory. The Braves would pitch Spahn and Johnny Sain, and pray for rain. We'd pitch Bobby game after game after game, with Dickie Farr behind the plate. He could hold onto Bobby's high, hard one, as well as the breaking ball, and a tank couldn't run him over at the plate.

Don Duncklee, at the hot corner, could fire the ball to first like a shot from an M-1 rifle, and I usually held onto it for a sure out.

Bob Kellar roamed the outfield with the gait of Dom DiMaggio, and Jim Emmert, although more at home with a basketball, did a good imitation of Billy Goodman of the Sox, who could play just about any position on the field. Bill Fortune, Dick Fisher, and David Clough, now a well-known artist in Maine rounded out what we considered at the time to be a team of All-Star status!

When the game was over, we'd head back to our home field, and maybe play a pickup game, or just sit in the grass by the tennis courts and watch the big guys slam balls around. Five of the best clay courts anywhere were rolled and nurtured to pool table flatness by Tony, and over the years some of the greatest players on the east coast tested their talents on the Newton Center courts. Don Manchester, a world-class player, and his cronies would have matches reminiscent of Longwood, Forest Hills and other national championship outings...right in the middle of Newton Center!

If it rained on your parade, you could always head for The Hut, a green-shingled building that looked more like a cottage at the beach than a basketball court. You opened the front door, and there you were at center court of a not-so-regulation round ball court that also over the years had some great players swishing shots from a floor that Tony babied as if it were the parquet at the old Boston Garden. Billy Fitz could shoot over the rafters from the shortened center court and hit nothing but net. Billy and his crew could have beaten the Celtics at The Hut.

The genius of Tony would also appear every Fourth of July. He and a special team would set up the fireworks display, and our hallowed grounds would explode with thunder and flashing light for thousands of people to "ooh and ahh" over. Then, by mid-morning of the next day, somehow all the holiday litter was gone, and the pristine acreage awaited our arrival.

The end of summer was always a shock to me. Those joyous days at the oasis passed in a flash, and the walk to Weeks Junior High School, and then Newton High, awaited. The only saving grace was that at least the snow would fly soon!

THE DAIRY FARM

In 1934 or 1935, our family moved from Boston to Hingham. My sister and I loved living a short walk from The Public Gardens and the Swan Boats, but now we were moving to the country. We couldn't wait to have our own yard to play in!

When the moving van pulled up to the beautiful little house on School Street, Sister and I were like two kids at an amusement park. Then for some reason, the movers spread three or four rugs out on the grass before starting to unload the boxes and furniture from the truck. For the next hour or so, we did somersaults on the rugs and laughed at our good fortune to be moving to the country.

Early the next morning, my father and I walked through a small field to the dairy farm next to our new yard. The barn behind the farmhouse was where the action was. A couple of dozen cows were inside the barn with two farmers doing the milking. There were no automatic milking machines in those days. It was just two men sitting on milking stools, squirting milk into pails.

I was fascinated with everything in that barn...the Holstein cows and the wonderful smell of the barn, a combination of hay, feed from a silo, and manure. To me, it was like perfume, and I never tired of that marvelous odor!

We waited until the milking was done, and my father introduced himself, and me, as the new neighbors. Mr. Kaparis owned the farm. His handyman, Harold Castle, who lived in a little cottage on the farm, was his jack-of-all-trades, as we found out in years to come.

Mr. Kaparis, a giant of a man, invited us in for breakfast. The large table in the kitchen was loaded with homemade muffins and rolls, eggs, bacon, ham, potatoes, and pancakes! I had never seen anything like it in my four years of living. Mr. Kaparis had a housekeeper/cook who ran the farmhouse like a bed and breakfast of today only the food was far better than any B&B that I would ever be in for the next seventy-five years!

Our new neighbor was from one of the Scandinavian countries, and spoke with a loud, accented voice. When we left that morning, he told my father and me that we were welcome for breakfast anytime, and invited me to help him in the barn if I wanted to. That was music to my young ears, and a great friendship was formed that wonderful day in the mid-30s.

Many a morning I walked over to the barn to do my chores and have breakfast. Mr. Kaparis gave me an old pair of rubber boots about six sizes too big for me. My favorite job was shoveling out the area where the cows were in their stanchions when they were in the barn. I even learned how to help with the milking now and then, and had my own milking stool. I sure wish I had that today, as it would be in a place of honor in our house!

Looking back to those days on the farm still gives me great joy. Mr. Kaparis didn't treat me like a four or five-year-old kid, and neither did Harold and May, the cook. I was one of them. I was treated as a grownup dairy farmer, and loved every minute of it.

Many years ago the farm was sold, and like small farms all over America, housing developments took over that beautiful landscape. The Mr. Kaparises of the world are few and far between now, and the wonderful smell of the dairy farm vanished along with the farms.

Oh, how lucky I was to be a dairy farmer those many years ago, and to meet all the people at the Kaparis' farm. That was an education for me that was far greater than I ever received in school!

THE CHOCOLATE HOUSE

On the other side of our home on School Street in Hingham was where Miss Studley lived. She was quite a bit older than our mother, but they became the greatest of friends.

Miss Studley taught school, and also taught piano at her house. What sticks out in my mind, though, is that she made the most delicious chocolates I have ever had in my life! You could take the most expensive chocolates in the world, do a taste test, and Miss Studley's would be the winner every time!

Sister and I called her house the chocolate house, and we spent a lot of time over there. When you entered, the smell of chocolate would hit you, and you were in heaven. The very large room in the back of the house had display cases full of various chocolates, and we were allowed to sample some on a regular basis. Miss Studley sold some right from the house, but also delivered some to select stores on the south shore of Boston. She had either a Model T Ford or maybe a Model A, but I think it was a T, and after packing up her car, off she'd go to make some deliveries.

My mother didn't drive and never did, so on many a Saturday she'd hop in the Model T with Miss Studley to take what they called "toots" all around the south shore and even down to Cape Cod. To drive to the Cape then was considered a long trip. Even in the cold weather they'd take touring blankets with them and bundle up for one of their "toots"!

Of course, the Depression was in full swing then, and many people had problems putting food on the table. Miss Studley wasn't one of those people, but since she lived alone she didn't spend a lot of time cooking for herself. Every Sunday, my mother would cook a T-bone steak for her, served with a large baked potato, and asparagus or green beans. Top this off with homemade bread pudding or gingerbread with whipped cream, and you had a great dinner!

Miss Studley knew I loved all the chocolates she made, but one in particular was my favorite...dark, rich chocolate with a creamed orange filling, which she called the orange delight. On my birthday, probably my fifth, she presented me with a pound of orange delights! I gave Sister a few, but ate over three-quarters of a pound myself within about a half an hour.

Life was sure good in the chocolate house!

THE GOOD OLD DAYS

In the 1930s and 1940s, the junkman, the bread man, the iceman, and the mailman were a part of everyday life for most of us.

When we lived on Free Street in Hingham during the late '30s, there was always a certain excitement in the air when the Cushman Bread truck would arrive at your driveway. The bread man would carry his huge tray of goodies to the front door, always making sure that the jelly rolls, doughnuts, and cakes were displayed well ahead of the bread.

He knew full-well that the kids of the house would immediately sing the hit song of the day, which by the way, never left the "Top 10" charts for as long as Sister and I could remember! Every kid we knew sang the same tune once or twice a week when the bread man appeared – "Mom, can we get jellyrolls?!" It had a great beat to it, and once in a while, Mom would reward the singers with jellyrolls or doughnuts!

Sister and I also perked up once or twice a week when the iceman pulled up in front with his huge truck. Our icebox sat in the back entryway and depended on the iceman to cool it down with a huge block of ice at each delivery. It was a big deal when we got an electric refrigerator in 1939 or so, but we sure missed the iceman.

On his delivery day, Mom would put the small sign in the window which showed the number "1", or, perhaps the "1/2" sign or even the "1/4" sign, depending on how much of the block of ice you needed. The burly iceman would grab his ice tongs, stab a huge block, throw it over his shoulder like it was a feather, and head for the icebox.

On a hot summer day, Sister would always escort me back out to the truck, knowing that the iceman would present us with a couple of large chips of coolness that he had from separating some of the blocks. There was nothing better than sitting under the pine tree with Sister on a hot summer day on Free Street with ice water dripping from your lips through that smile of contentment!

The milkman even brought a little excitement with him when *he* arrived. Mr. Honstra, from his farm down the road, would deliver the milk, and put it in the icebox. As he took back the empty bottles to the truck, we followed, and he, too, would give us a handful of ice chips on a hot day. Then, it was back to the house to check on the cream!

The milk wasn't homogenized then, so the cream would rise to the top of the bottle and stay there. Perhaps, Mom would make gingerbread that day and remove the cream from the milk bottle to make whipped cream! That may not ring with excitement for today's kids, but let me tell you, homemade whipped cream, made by Sister and my mother, over hot gingerbread excited me to no end!

The Coal Man would visit in the cold months fairly often, and run a slide down into the coal bin in the cellar, setting us up for a few weeks of heat. The old saying back then was, "If you're not a good kid, Santa Claus will only leave you a stick and a piece of coal for Christmas."

Every time our Coal Man came to our house he'd say, "You'd better be good or Santa will pick up some coal from me to serve you for Christmas!" We'd laugh hysterically, and so would he. We never tired of him saying that.

The Mailman was practically a member of the family. Our mailman's name was Harold, the same as our father's, and we were allowed to call him by his first name, as he always wanted us to. The mailmen all walked their routes then, and they took the post office saying to heart – "Through snow, sleet, rain, heat, and cold, the U.S. mail must go through." (Something like that anyhow.) On many a day, my mother would serve the mailman a glass of water, hot chocolate, or even a slice of jellyroll, if we had any. After all, Harold was a member of our family!

Then, you always had door-to-door salesmen calling. The Fuller Brush Man had his route and would always leave some little item for free – maybe a vegetable brush, or something similar. My sister cherished her Fuller Brush hairbrush, and we were always glad to see The Fuller Brush Man arrive. On many days, my mother never bought anything, but he called on us for years.

The junkman, in his old beat up truck, was the same in Newton as he was in Hingham. It wasn't the same man, but they operated the same way – slow drive by, ringing a bell to summon those with parcels of "whatever" was how they operated. We had moved to Newton Center in 1941, and Sister, being a smart businesswoman, saved "stuff" for the junkman.

You never threw anything away because the junkman wasn't called that for no reason. He'd buy anything! You'd see sleds, baby carriages, chairs, tires, bikes, etc., hanging from his truck, but his biggest business was newspapers. Everyone tied up their newspapers in small bales, and the junkman would weigh them and, supposedly, pay you accordingly. Sister loved to collect newspapers, bale them, and stack them in the cellar next to the coal bin. (Yes, we had a coal man too!)

The house on Pleasant Street sat on top of the hill, and it was quite a hike up that hill to the back of the house and bulkhead to the basement. Sister's paper collection had reached six feet in height and surrounded the coal bin. It was junkman time! Sister escorted the man to the basement and followed him to the truck with each load to check the weight on the scale, which hung off the back of the truck. Then, they made the trek back up to the house for another stack of papers.

There had always been rumors that the junkman was of the Enron and Big American Business School. Shall we just be kind and say "unethical"? My friend, David Clough, and I had what we thought was a great idea, and proceeded to put our business plan into effect without telling our C.E.O., Sister, what our stroke of genius was!

As Sister and Mr. Junkman trudged back and forth up the hill to the basement, David and I took bales of newspapers from a different pile on the truck, ran up and around the other side of the house, and piled them on the other side of the coal bin! We did this with great glee for a time, until on one trip Sister had stayed in the basement for some reason, and stared at us as we carried newspapers back into the basement!

In my mind, Sister was as honest as the day is long, as she in fact was, so I stuttered and stammered explaining why we were giving the junkman some of his own medicine! Sister looked at me in disbelief, paused for what seemed a full couple of minutes, and said, "Jackie, that's a wonderful idea, but let's only do it with a dozen or so more bundles!!"

The junkman paid Sister and left, probably thinking he had once again bilked some kids out of some cash! David and I walked up to Morgan Brother's Creamery in Newton Center square, and blew the money Sister had presented to us on one ice cream after another! At dinner that evening our mother and father asked how things went with the junkman. Sister made many points for me when she said, "Jackie and David went out of their way to help me!"

Over the years, Sister and I would embellish on the junkman story, and laugh the laugh of eleven and twelve-year-old kids!

Those were great days, and you were friends with all deliverymen. Things aren't as friendly today, and I'm glad to have those memories in The Bank.

THE COOP

The Reverend Martin Luther King had a dream. His dream was the beginning of change for the better for African-Americans and other citizens alike. My dream of a few nights ago although just as vivid as the Reverend's didn't change the lives of millions. However, my dream took me back to 1941 through 1945 or 1946, and it sure added a lot to the lives of some young boys in Newton Center, Massachusetts. Perhaps my dream, at age 78, was only for a few minutes, but it might as well have been hours, and it was great to be age 10 through 15 again!

The Coop was a stand-alone, oversized, one-car garage on Pleasant Street in Newton Center. If garages were listed by real estate brokers, the copy would have been something like this:

Sitting on a slight hill, with a winding driveway, this oversized, one-car garage is a thing of beauty! Although only 25 yards from the main house, it's as if it was half a mile away...a "get away," if you will! This masterpiece won't last long, so drive up the hill and check it out. A steal at $400.00!"

Remember, you could buy a four-bedroom house for four or five grand!

I don't remember how it happened, but one day when I was 10 or 11, the garage became The Coop. It was my home away from home, yet close enough to smell breakfast, lunch, and dinner being prepared in the kitchen of the house. It sort of appeared with the snap of a couple of fingers. Jimmy Emmert and I set up a couple of cots, a few orange crates, and we went from there.

My father was content to leave the car, a 1937 Ford "woodie" station wagon outside, and The Coop was ours! The Coop was the best house Jimmy and I, and our other

53

"Coop" associates ever lived in! There was no mortgage, no taxes, no electric bill, no anything… just pleasure!

In no time at all, we had Varga Girls on the wall from *Esquire Magazine*, as well as all the Boston Red Sox player photos, street signs from around Newton, baseball cards, etc. The orange crates were used for seats, storing comic books, *Big Little Books*, and *National Geographic*…the wonderful, yellow-covered gems that usually had bare-breasted natives on a number of pages!

Our cigar boxes were loaded with Fatima and Wings cigarettes (from Jim's father's collection), and a few cigars, corncob pipes, and yes, a crate with even a couple of beers and occasionally, a bottle of Caldwell's Rum (again, from Jim's father's liquor cabinet!). Caldwell's didn't occupy space for too long, as I got deathly sick from my experiments with hard stuff, and it was banned from The Coop…not by my parents, but by Jimmy and me!

You didn't need a membership to enter The Coop – no membership card, no interview by a committee, and surely no dues. However, it was just assumed, without any official ceremony, that a select few could come and go as they wished. They might as well have had the words The Coop tattooed on the inside of their arm that was put there at birth because they were special!

Since Jimmy lived only about 300 yards from the establishment, and I was only about twenty-five yards away, we were sort of the custodians of the place, and slept many a night in the house that Jimmy and Jack built! There was never a roll call, but guys would just show up, and the floor was always open for discussion. When the full congregation was on hand, laughter could be heard for hours. No computers, computer games, cell phones, adults, etc…just young kids enjoying whatever came about.

In later years, I learned in the Marine Corps that Marines take care of each other at all times. Well, we of

"The Coop" years did the same thing. No one ever walked the plank alone. If one went off the plank, we all did. Donnie Duncklee, Bobby Gregory, Dave Clough, Dickie Farr, Billy Fortune, Neil Bridges, Bobby Kellar, Bill Ripley, Ted Ripley, and Bobby's brother, Sonny, were the mainstays of the crew. Our years at The Coop were like the Master Card ads…PRICELESS!

The '37 Ford was parked outside, and became the personal after dark vehicle for Jimmy and me to travel in around the streets of Newton late at night. My father had taught me how to drive when I was about thirteen! The ignition switch for the wagon was on the steering column, and included a switch you'd push up after putting the key in. However, my father always took the key out without locking the switch, so we were free to travel…sort of our own Hertz Rent-a-Car with no paper work!

Over a period of a month or so, I taught Jimmy how to drive! He drove over a few lawns and yellow lines, but he was a fast learner. I issued him a verbal certificate to drive after he passed the test of slowly driving up the driveway at night… no lights, no noise… to put the wagon to sleep for the night! That, of course, was after putting fifty cents worth of gas in the tank. In later years, I thought my Dad actually left the switch unlocked, and knew every move we made! He never told me so, but it wouldn't have surprised me!

In looking back through the years, I realize how lucky we were to grow up in the '30s and '40s! Yeah, I know, I sound like an old guy living in the past, and thinking the old days were far superior to today's world. Well, with me, that's it in a nutshell! We didn't have cell phones, laptops, beepers, Blackberries, Google, Facebook, TV…and hundreds of other conveniences of today. But we did have The Coop, and wonderful friends to fill it on a rainy day or any other day!

We traveled on our own route without much supervision. From dawn to dusk, we enjoyed life without much input from adults in our free time. We did our own thing, and loved every minute of it! We didn't miss out on those years of pure enjoyment…oh, how lucky we were!

The Coop still stands on top of the little hill at 112 Pleasant Street, Newton Center, Massachusetts. I'm hoping that some kid has his own "Coop" behind that garage door, but I'm afraid it has been more silent than a library over the past 60 years. Perhaps the owners of 112 Pleasant Street would rent The Coop to me for one final reunion!

Those of us who are still around could sit on orange crates and laugh about the old days! Dunk, Dickie, Jimmy, Bobby K., Dave, Sonny, and even a few "junior members" would open the meeting with a toast to those who are not with us in person anymore, but surely in spirit…Bobby Gregory, Neil Bridges, Bill and Ted Ripley, and a handful of others who used to drop by now and then.

Whoever said, "Grown men don't cry" is nuts! We'd all have tears in our eyes, but tears of joy. The Coop truly had its own personality, and there's a piece of The Coop in every one of us who was fortunate enough to enter!

THE SHOW MUST GO ON

In the summer of 1942 or 1943, Sister and her friend, Patsy Merrick, who lived a few houses away from us in Newton Center, caught the actress/director bug! They'd read various plays together, act out some of the parts, and I think they thought they would eventually hit the big time. They knew, however, that you had to gain experience in front of an actual audience to earn your spurs as a real actor. Deciding to write, produce, and direct their own three-person play was a beginning. Polly Henan, who lived across from Patsy, would be the supporting actress to the two stars.

They approached me, or I should say demanded that I sit down and listen to their idea. The wonderful detached garage at our Pleasant Street house was practically where I lived. It was clubhouse, bunkhouse, and funhouse, but not a playhouse for an amateur thespian production! However, with a few words from Sister, I was persuaded easily into being the stage manager, ticket manager, usher, P.R. director, and janitor for the new "Pleasant Street Players"! "My" garage, known fondly as The Coop, would now be a summer playhouse for Sister and her actress friends!

Their original one-act play had to do with three women from the 1920s era, who summered together at Nantasket Beach in one of the beautiful old homes that used to be at the lower end of the beach. I can't recall the name of the play, and not much of the theme. However, I do remember they somehow came up with old-fashioned, long dresses, wore a lot of makeup, and desperately tried to speak as though they were well along in years!

They made up tickets by cutting up index cards, and made cardboard posters for me to nail up at the playground and light poles here and there. It was decided that ten cents was a little steep for a show of that kind, so the magic number was seven. A kid could scrape together seven cents somehow, and fork it over for a late afternoon extravaganza at The Playhouse.

They rehearsed the whole month of July. We set up a pull-curtain in the garage from a sheet, and orange crates (which were plentiful at the grocery stores then) would seat two people. I can remember really getting into this upcoming Academy Award performance, and I promoted and sold tickets to everyone I knew. Those friends told other friends and, as opening night approached in mid-August, we figured that the overflowing crowd would be standing room only in the driveway!

The afternoon of the performance showed our cigar box cash register brimming over with cash from advance sales, and there would be more to come from show goers who hadn't paid in advance. Curtain call was for five o'clock, and we couldn't believe the number of kids who were waiting to applaud or boo. We didn't know which. However, we'd soon find out.

At 5:20, the curtain hadn't moved, and the audience was screaming! I went "backstage," and there sat Patsy Merrrick in tears…stage fright had taken over big time. She couldn't even speak, let alone imitate an older woman! Polly pulled the "Well, if Patsy can't do it, I sure can't!" excuse, and they huddled in the corner listening to the jeering crowd. Sister seemed even calmer than she usually was as she contemplated the situation.

"Jackie, take the cigar box and put it out the back window. Now, go out and tell the audience we're very sorry, but Patsy and Polly, two of the stars, are too sick to perform. Tell them their tickets are rain checks for the next performance, which will be held before school starts!"

Now I know how General Custer must have felt when he saw and heard all those Indians screaming at him! Somehow I yelled out Sister's instructions, and the place slowly emptied. In the days that followed, the disaster turned into just another fun happening. All the kids commented about how much fun it was looking forward to the play, and when they got there how much fun it was to see so many kids they knew in one place at the same time. It became a wonderful conversation piece for weeks!

Sister never did write/direct/or star in another play. However, she became a *superstar* in the "Theater of Life"! The money in the cigar box? Sister decided to split it four ways. Patsy and Polly did their best, and I carried out my end of the deal. Sister also said the kids all got their money's worth anyhow. For only seven cents they got to see all of their school friends while on vacation, and had a great story to talk about for, perhaps, years to come!

I guess that's what show business is all about!

WWII RATIONING

In early January of 1942, practically everything you were used to getting for everyday life was rationed. Only a handful of items weren't, and they were things you hardly ever bought!

The first thing that comes to my mind is margarine. I knew rationing had hit our home when my mother would stir yellow coloring into the margarine we used to make it look like butter! Every package of margarine came with a color packet! Very seldom did we have real butter for about three years.

Of course, the biggest and most important cutback for families during the war was gasoline. Each family had a ration book for gasoline and there were three categories of gas ration cards – A, B, and C. Whatever group you were in was put on your windshield with a sticker. The "A" card/coupon was worth only four gallons a week – "B" was worth six gallons, and "C" eight gallons. My father was classified as "C" because he was a contractor and had to use his vehicle more than most.

When you got gas you had to use your coupon book and hand it to the man or woman who pumped the gas. Many women worked in the gas stations as so many men were drafted or joined the military.

Tires were impossible to get, and the only ones available were retreads. Retreads then were dangerous to use, so maybe it was a blessing in disguise that no one drove that much!

Sugar, coffee, meat, chicken, and dozens of other items were hard to come by, as were cigarettes, pipe tobacco, chocolate, and practically everything else. But ya know, I never remember any true hardship because of the rationing. It was a patriotic effort by everyone to cut down across the board, and we did so without much complaining as I remember.

My father had a guy who worked for him that was a part-time cook at the Manger Hotel in Boston. He would appear once in awhile with butter or beef and sell it to people on the job. My Dad would never buy it, and told the guy not to even bring anything on the job anymore.

From 1942 to late 1945, there were no new cars made. All production at auto plants was for military vehicles, and anything used in the war. The first new cars were in 1946.

Along with rationing, I remember War Bonds. All the kids would have a War Bond booklet, and purchase stamps for twenty-five cents each to fill the book. When you got to $18.75, you tucked the book away and in ten years it would be worth $25.00. My sister, Ann, and I had a War Bond book, and proudly put a stamp in each week if we could!

Along with the rationing came the Civil Defense Act. Men and women would volunteer to spend time policing neighborhoods to enforce the new safety regulations. Every house had to have blackout curtains or blackout shutters so if nighttime bombings ever hit America, the countryside would be as dark as possible. Luckily, unlike England, we never had that horrible problem. Each volunteer received a flashlight, helmet and nightstick. My father was a group leader in our neighborhood.

Everyone saved newspapers, tin cans, aluminum foil from cigarette packages, or wherever else you found it. Everything was turned in for use in the war effort!

I'll never forget helping my father paint half of the car headlights black, so if you had to drive at night the lights wouldn't be as bright for enemy aircraft to see. The beaches were patrolled by the Coast Guard, Navy, and

Army, many with watchdogs at their side. German submarines were seen off the coast of Cape Cod, and other parts of the East Coast. They actually caught a small band of Germans coming ashore to infiltrate the area as spies!

You know, the war was a horrible thing, but looking back, it was incredible how everyone pitched in and pulled together to do whatever possible for the war effort. The atmosphere was one of high patriotism, as we all felt we were playing a part in winning the war and helping our military survive.

Times change, and I'm afraid not for the better. It seems that attitudes have changed drastically. We're not anywhere near as cordial as we used to be. People don't seem to go out of their way for others like they used to. Many will say I'm just a grumpy old man living in the past. Well, maybe I am, but I don't think the younger people of today will have as many wonderful memories in their Memory Bank as we old grumpy people do! That is, unless we make some changes, and go back to some of the things we did in the '30s, '40s, and '50s!

Okay, I'm off my soapbox, and heading up to the gas station with my coupon book! Filling my tank will cost fifty bucks. In 1946, it cost three bucks. Eat your heart out!

CHRISTMAS CAROLS

In the early 1940s, the Christmas season wasn't complete unless it happened to snow, as it did often. Many of the sidewalks in Newton were plowed by wonderful workhorses pulling a "V"-shaped plow through the snow. Some of the horses even had a few bells attached to their harness, which gave the whole scene a Norman Rockwell look, and we loved it.

The frosting on the Christmas cake was when the carolers would come by in the evening, and with their Christmas spirit and beautiful voices send a cheerful message to all of us that Christmas was really upon us! The bundled up singers in groups of a dozen or so, would perform in front of your house, and move slowly through the neighborhood spreading their good will. Many of the fortunate recipients of the caroling would serve them hot chocolate or hot cider, and the ritual always made my sisters and me extra excited about the upcoming big day!

Our mother and father always told us that one of the greatest gifts in life were the small things that really touched your heart. Well, the carolers with their great enthusiasm, and winter breath dancing in the cold air, gave us that wonderful present in the 1940s. Every Christmas, I think back to those great days of being a kid of ten or eleven-years-old, and if I close my eyes, I can see those carolers standing on the newly plowed sidewalks sending cheer to all of us.

Whoever said, "Some of the best things in life are free" had it right. There was no money involved in the true spirit of Christmas, and the carolers reminded us of that. We need more of that in today's world!

BOSTON

Back in the 1940s, for a kid growing up in the Boston area, there were certain levels you had to reach if you wanted to be certified as a true Bostonian. You had to have a flair for wandering off the straight and narrow path of life, for what fun is it to travel on the paved highways all the time? Ya gotta hit the side streets, the dirt roads – the establishments where the real people live!

If you were fortunate enough, let's say at the age of about twelve, to be hanging around with a few friends that had adventure in their hearts, you could begin working on collecting merit badges in life that would stay with you forever. I happened to be one of the lucky ones that took advantage of every opportunity to earn a degree in life that had nothing to do with a classroom!

From about the age of nine, I was fortunate to live in Newton Center, Massachusetts, within a half-mile or so of a half dozen boys my age, who more or less had the same desire to investigate life to the fullest. The Newton Schools, at that time, were rated near the top in the country, but what was in our hearts, you didn't learn in school.

In junior high school, we all walked the mile and a half or more to school. The same route each day took us around Crystal Lake, across the railroad tracks to Weeks Junior High School. We swam in Crystal Lake, played hockey at Crystal Lake, snuck cigarettes and even a beer at Crystal Lake, but the best part of Crystal Lake was our annual rite of spring. In very early April, with thin ice still floating in the water, we'd strip down to our "birthday suits" and jump through the ice! It was heaven because that meant that in a couple of months school would be out for the summer!

The Boston Red Sox and Fenway Park beckoned! The bleachers at Fenway were the place to be. Twenty-five cents for a double-header, peanuts for five cents a bag, and memories were priceless! Ted Williams, Dom DiMaggio, Bobby Doerr…we loved every minute of it!

One of the joys of life for me was skipping school. There was something about it that really turned me on. School and I didn't get along, but it wasn't just that. It was the thrill of just going against the system, I guess. Heading for Scolley Square in Boston was like a trip to heaven for us! It was where all the sailors from the Boston Navy Yard would go for liberty…where there were more bars and penny arcades than anywhere in the state…and last, but not least, the burlesque shows!

The Old Howard and the Casino had strippers that would make a kid want to skip school every day and head for the Square! Peaches, Queen of Shake, Ann Corio, Lilly Ann Rose, Sally Rand, and dozens of others were never anywhere near naked, but the eyes of a fourteen or fifteen-year-old kid were different from adults. They sure seemed naked to us!

Scolley Square was the cause of my skipping school five days in a row! I had heard about truant officers, but never believed there really was one. Well, there was, and he appeared at our house on the evening of my fifth day of freedom. My mother was the disciplinarian in our family. My father was very laid back and never got overly excited about my shenanigans. What a guy he was! My mother went to school with me and she and the principal decided that detention was the ticket for me – an hour after school each day in study hall.

Months later, my mother visited the principal to see how I was doing, and how my attendance was, etc.

When answering how my attendance was, Dr. Drake, the principal, said, "It's fine, Mrs. Orth. John only takes the regular holidays off…Thanksgiving, Christmas, school vacation, and the Jewish holidays."

My mother was shocked, and told him we weren't Jewish, and once again, I was in big trouble!

We sneaked cigarettes when we had them. When not, we smoked corn silk, pine needles, or even tea in a corncob pipe! When we could get beer, it was Pickwick Ale, called poor man's whiskey. We rode our bikes everywhere. We raked leaves, shoveled snow, mowed lawns, had paper routes, and always seemed to have a nickel in our pockets when needed. We had the time of our lives. We were free as birds on the wing, and we all turned out pretty well!

My father, on many occasions, when I would do things a little out of the ordinary, would say with a twinkle in his eye, "Jackson, sometimes I just don't understand you!"

In my own way, I took that as a compliment!

THE DRIVER'S LICENSE

Rating the number one event in a person's life is next to impossible, but there are a handful of things that, let's say, tie for first place. One of those "firsts" happened for me on a snowy day in 1947 in Newton, Massachusetts.

As the snow deepened an inch or two every hour on that December day, I made a life-changing deposit in my Memory Bank! I had just turned sixteen, and was set to take the driving test so I could drive legally on the highways and byways of Massachusetts. For practically two years, I had taken a spin on those roads without a license, but those days would be over!

Excitement ruled at our house in Newton Center that day. Off we'd go to the Registry of Motor Vehicles in Waltham for my driving test in our 1937 Ford "woodie" station wagon. The marvelous wonder with the stick shift on the floor had served our family through the World War II years, and was ready for retirement. However, no mission it had ever encountered was as important as forging through the snow to get to Waltham on time for the most important test drive ever in the life of a sixteen-year-old kid!

Whenever my father really wanted me to pay close attention to what he said, my name, Jack, was transformed to Jackson.

"Jackson, the Registry may be closed because of the storm, making it impossible for them to handle a test drive today. Calling them on the phone would undoubtedly guarantee a 'we'll have to reschedule your appointment to a later date' response. We'll just drive over there and take a chance on just showing up early!"

The average father would have thought better of driving twenty miles in a blizzard to be turned down for an appointment, but that never entered my father's mind.

There is a decision that has a gold star beside it in my Memory Bank. I'll never forget the wonderful ring to his voice, and the smile on his face as he practically bellowed, "Let's get going, Jackson!"

Nobody was at the Registry...well, almost nobody. A woman was behind the counter, and a tall, uniformed Registry officer announced they were just about ready to close up shop.

My father, in his best calm manner, set the stage by saying, "Sir, we drove over from Newton Center, and driving wasn't really too bad." For a few seconds, in what seemed like five minutes, you could have heard a pin drop.

A slight smile appeared on the officer's face as he questioned, "Do you have chains on your automobile?"

"No, we don't Officer, but I'm sure we can get a set nearby, and put them on," answered my father.

"If you can get back here in ten or fifteen minutes, we'll give it a try," came the terrific reply.

Hardware stores carried sets of four chains. You strapped two units on each back wheel, and for short distances they worked fairly well. We were back at the Registry in no time and ready to go.

With me at the wheel, my father in the back, and the officer riding "shot gun," I was instructed to drive down the street, turn right, drive to the stop sign, turn right, drive to the stop sign, turn right, drive to the stop sign, turn right, and pull up in front of the Registry.

There were, of course, no directional signals in a '37 "woodie." You'd wind down the window rain or shine, snow or sleet, and do the appropriate left-arm signal. All of this and a half-mile or so test drive (perhaps the shortest in Massachusetts history) was done with the ease of a kid who had secretly driven hundreds of miles without the proper credentials for quite some time!

The Registry of Motor Vehicle officer has a reserved spot in my Memory Bank, too. Not in the box seats in the first row with my father, but he does enjoy an incredible view of the playing field.

What a day that was! I drove home with the bumping of the chains and the slapping of the chain straps playing a tune of utter joy, as my father said, "Jackson, let's stop in Newton Corner for a nice lunch at George's Café!"

THE PINK SLIP

For thousands of people over the years, a "pink slip" was a piece of paper you never wanted to see. The dreaded "pink slip" was something put in your paycheck envelope on Friday that stated your services were no longer needed – you were fired…let go…canned!

However, for a sixteen-year-old kid in Massachusetts, a pink slip was your ticket to paradise. Your pass to the freedom-trail of life. The highway to happiness was yours to drive on, and it was toll free. You could pass through the gate legally… you had your driver's license!

Like many happenings in life, certain goals when reached also contain a small asterisk barely visible to the naked eye! The small print on your cherished pink slip stated: TEMPORARY…WITHIN THIRTY DAYS YOU WILL RECEIVE YOUR PERMANENT AUTOMOBILE LICENSE. ANY TRAFFIC VIOLATION BEFORE THE ISSUE OF THAT DOCUMENT MAY RESULT IN FORFEITURE OF YOUR DRIVING PRIVILEGES UNTIL A LATER DATE.

"Who cares? Thirty days is nothing. All I know is I can drive anywhere I want to!" Famous last words.

Delivering a small load of insulation to my father's crew at a job in Watertown was great fun, and I had traveled the delivery route before, but this time legally! On the way back, just short of Watertown Square on Mt. Vernon Street, I passed a trolley car, which in the 1940s used Mt. Vernon just as the cars did. Passing a trolley on the left wasn't permitted. However, many did and the rule wasn't heavily enforced, but it sure was on this beautiful, clear day in January of 1946!

The Watertown cop pulled me over and asked for my license and registration. Taking the pink slip from my wallet sent a lightening bolt-like shot of fear through my mind, and directly to my very heart! *I can't get a ticket! I might not get my permanent license!*

"Sir, I just made a delivery of insulation, and I'm returning another load. I wasn't thinking. I'm sorry. I'm driving on a pink slip, Sir. Please don't issue me a ticket!"

The big, Irish-looking cop replied, "Get out of your car. I noticed your right brake light don't work, and the glass is broke." We both looked at the taillight, and he said once again, "It don't work, and it's broke!"

I wasn't quite sure what to say, and I sort of just repeated what he had said, "It doesn't work and it's broken?"

"What are you? Some kind of wise kid?" yelled the cop.

Somehow, I realized in a flash that he thought I was correcting his English, and I replied, "No! No! I can see it don't work and the glass is broke!"

His demeanor changed immediately, and I almost wanted to hug him as he said, "Okay, okay, I'm not writing up a faulty equipment report. Do you guarantee me you'll have this light fixed in a day or so?"

I thanked him from the bottom of my heart, and of course told him I'd have the "broke" light repaired right away, and I did! The '37 Ford "woodie" wagon don't have a broke taillight no more!

THE PAPER ROUTE

One of the rites of passage in the 1940s was for a young kid to try his hand at the honorable job of delivering the paper. In those days, many newspapers had a morning and evening edition. Remember, there was no TV, Internet, etc., and many of us grouchy old seniors wish nothing ever changed from those days. Whenever I see ten-year-old kids with cell phones, beepers, Blackberries, Blueberries, Raspberries, whatever, the same thought runs through my mind – "You poor little bastards! Someone knows where you are every minute of the day! Your life ain't your own!"

Hmm…I digress…back to the route. The newspaper distribution office was on Union Street in Newton Center. I had a morning route, and would ride my bike to the office, fold my papers into the "throwing" mode, and take off with my bag over my shoulder to deliver the news of the day. A guy named Charlie Hall and his sister (Phyllis, I think) ran the office. They ruled with an iron fist, but we all liked them anyhow.

Some houses you couldn't just throw the papers up to the door – too far – way too far. That was "a carry to the door" delivery. I shall never forget one of my "throwing" deliveries. A good paperboy could fold the paper firmly and use a Frisbee motion with great accuracy. One morning just as I made the perfect throw, the lady of the house opened the door, the paper hit a vase on a small table inside the house, and the vase hit the floor in pieces. I was shocked and scared to death that my route days were over.

Turns out the lady took it in stride, and she wouldn't hear of me replacing the vase or paying for it. She said it was just one of those things that happens that really isn't anyone's fault. I have a strange feeling that in today's world that could have spelled lawsuit. My mother and father suggested I bring the lady some tomatoes and squash from our Victory Garden. I did, and I made a friend. Funny what a little thoughtfulness will do.

Soon, I graduated to delivery and selling magazines – *Colliers*, *Saturday Evening Post*, and I think, *Look Magazine*. I can't remember how much money we made from the various routes – not a lot – but I always seemed to have a couple of nickels to rub together. A dime would buy a model airplane kit or two candy bars or a half-gallon of gas when I "borrowed" my father's car.

I just filled my gas tank this morning for $3.15 per gallon! I love my Memory Bank – you sure could get a lot for a dime!

MIDNIGHT RIDES

Long before being blessed by the Commissioner of Motor Vehicles with the life changing "pink slip," we were able to frequent the roads of the Commonwealth of Massachusetts in my father's wonderful wooden chariot! The station wagons of the 1930s and '40s weren't called station wagons, they were called "Beach Wagons" in New England, and many a family headed for the shore in those wonderful vehicles.

For a fourteen-year-old kid, heading to the beach was great, but couldn't compare with late night rides around Newton in the 1937 Ford "woodie" Beach Wagon! The ignition lock was on the steering column, which also included an up and down switch to turn the car on and off. The key unlocked the switch box, and you pushed the switch to the "on" position to start the car. My father always took the key out of the ignition lock, but never turned it before doing so. In other words, he didn't actually lock the switch. You could flip it to the "on" position and away you'd go!

People of that marvelous era didn't have TV, so late night entertainment didn't keep them from practicing the "Early to bed, early to rise" motto of the work force of America. My parents were believers in the early sack time routine, and I loved the "sneak out of the house at 11 p.m. to drive the beach wagon" routine, and practiced it frequently! The "no key necessary" option was just an invitation to excitement that I couldn't turn down!

My great life-long friend, Jim Emmert usually rode shotgun with me, as he lived a few houses away and craved the challenge of the adventure as much as I did. The act of putting the car in neutral and coasting down the curved, hill driveway to the street was a thing of beauty! Then, with a flip of the switch, we were off to "freedomsville" for an hour or two!

The Howard Johnson's in Chestnut Hill was open until one in the morning. The Sunspot in Cleveland Circle was open all night. There's something about eating a hot dog or a burger when you're more or less "on the lam" that turns the snack into a meal fit for a king!

The route to the Sunspot took us past Boston College and the reservoir close by. The eleven to midnight crowds of boy/girl visitors would pack the street curving around the reservoir, and attendance was always high at what was known as B.C. Night School! Behind steamed-up car windows, America's leaders of the future were all studying "anatomy," and the hands-on experience would lead to many a diploma in physiology at B.C. Night School.

We'd laugh as we drove around the reservoir heading for Commonwealth Avenue and the route the Boston Marathon runners took into Cleveland Circle. Little did we know that a few years later we, too, would apply for a degree from B.C. Night School. We didn't exactly make the "Dean's List," but did anyone really fail altogether on those hallowed grounds?!

I may have been the youngest driving instructor in the state in the wagon, as Jimmie, a year younger than me, became my first pupil to receive his after-hours permit to drive. Our driving school route was the Oak Hill section of Newton, and the lawn of a large home near the Charles River Country Club may still have Good Year imprints on it from a wayward u-turn by Jimmie!

In later years, Jim was associated with General Motors, and was also involved in their racing program. He drove up Pike's Peak at an extremely fast rate of speed with the Indianapolis Speedway winner, Al Unser. Jim attributes his skills, and fearlessness of a few episodes with Unser, to his days of driving in Oak Hill!!

Before returning our wonderful wooden horse to the barn after our rides, we'd gas up at a Merit gas station. At seventeen cents a gallon we'd always spring for fifty cents, which would just about bring the tank back to where it was before rolling down the driveway on those exciting nights.

I never really discussed the midnight trips with my father, not even in much later years. But you know, before the "pink slip" arrived, he let me drive on many occasions when he needed something delivered to his insulation crews.

I always loved it when he'd off handedly say, "Jackson, do you want to run over to Hyde Park, and pick up some insulation and take it over to the job in Malden?" (or Watertown or wherever).

Perhaps he knew about our evening adventures, and just didn't interfere. However, I do know one thing – those wonderful nights are in my Memory Bank, and the interest they've drawn over the years is worth a lot more than any present bank is paying!

THE EGG WITH THE HOLE IN IT

In 1942, maybe 1943, I was invited by Louie Hurxthal to spend a week at their summer home in Plymouth. Louie was a couple of years older than me and lived in our neighborhood in good old Newton Center. The Hurxthals had one of the oldest houses in Plymouth, and it was only a short walk to the ocean, so we had a great time.

My first morning there, we sat down for breakfast. The Hurxthals had a French maid, and she was the greatest. She served us something I had never seen or heard of. She cut a circle out of a slice of bread, buttered both sides of the bread, put it in a frying pan, dropped an egg in the hole and cooked it just like a fried egg! She also toasted the little bread circles in the same pan. For five days I must have eaten at least a dozen of those wonderful treats for breakfast.

Louie and I had a great week with his Plymouth friends, and when I got home my mother asked me to tell her what the best part of my trip to Plymouth was. I told her I had a great time, but the best thing of all was the "French eggs"! For some reason I called it the egg with the hole in it, and have ever since. I've made hundreds of them for our kids over the years, and to this day our youngest, Wendy, now in her 40s, asks for an egg with a hole in it when she comes over!

Now, do a fast forward to around 1969 or so. We moved from Duxbury down to Plymouth and bought a great old house right around the corner from the Hurxthal house. In fact, their land butted up against ours. The French cook was no longer there, but the Hurxthals were. In later years Dr. Hurxthal retired, and he and his wife lived next door. The Doctor headed up the Leahy Clinic for many years, and was very well-known in the medical circles. I only tell you that for the following reason.

I'm mowing my lawn one day and the good doctor is walking past our house toward the ocean with his dog, Cosmo. I wave and turn off the mower as he walks by our front walk. On that walk sits a large twenty-four ounce plastic glass, which I pick up and take a drink from.

The Doctor was a very serious minded man, and in an all business way said,"What's that you're drinking?"

I told him it was a health drink, which I always called that wonderful mixture.

In his same serious tone he asked, "What's in it?"

I told him, "You fill the glass almost to the top with ice cubes, pour in four ounces of vodka, add orange juice and a touch of club soda, and you have a health drink. Would you like one?"

Without skipping a beat he said, "I believe I would!"

We went in the back by our small swimming pool and sat in the shade guzzling a couple of health drinks. Dr. H. told me that his wife, Dorothy, met friends in Boston many a Wednesday, had lunch and then went to the matinee of the theater. Then, in an extremely friendly way, he asked if I was off on Wednesdays, and would I mind if he visited again. I, of course, told him he was welcome any day, but if I was around on a Wednesday that would work for me!

He didn't come over often, but we became friends, which was great. Here I was serving health drinks to the retired head of the Leahy Clinic next door to where I learned how to make an egg with a hole in it!

Ah, ya had to be there I guess, but it sure is a valuable deposit in my Memory Bank!

COLBIANI SIGILLUM COLLEGI

The large, white pottery Colby College beer mug sits on my desk with the blue insignia sending memories my way. Since I failed Latin in school, the wording on the mug meant nothing to me on that Christmas morning of 1949, but the gift has always brought a smile to my face, and a nice jumpstart to my heart on many occasions.

Sister was a college freshman at Colby, and the chilly Christmas weather in Newton Center was practically summer to her. When she left Waterville, Maine, for the holiday vacation, it hovered around the zero degree mark, and would go below that magic number before she left.

Bobby Gregory and I knew full well the perils of Waterville in December. A few weeks before Santa's visit, on the spur of the moment, we decided to hop a bus in Park Square and make a visit to Sister for the weekend. The wind coming from The Public Gardens and The Common should have carried the message to us to stay put in the relative comfort of forty degrees or so in Boston. Of course, the last thing on a kid's mind is the weather, so the long bus ride was the order of the day as far as we were concerned.

Also, not being up on polite protocol, we arrived in Waterville unannounced. We proceeded to Mayflower Hill to find Sister. Stepping off the bus was like walking into a freezer at the butcher shop! The temperature was around zero, and walking to Mayflower qualified Bobby and me to join Admiral Byrd on his treks to the tundra!

Unannounced meant nothing to Sister! She was close to overjoyed to see us, which pleased me no end, as I wasn't quite sure how two high school kids would be welcomed to the grownup world of college! Within the hour, Sister, her roommate from New Jersey, and Bobby and I entered a café back downtown called Oney's to celebrate our arrival.

It was *the* place for the college kids, and pitchers of beer and pizza were the meal of choice. We were in heaven, and just about every moment of not sacking out on the floor of the dorm was spent at Oney's! If this was college, I figured I sure as hell had better start turning in homework, if that was the ticket to paradise.

The trip back was spent sleeping, and I'm sure with dreams of returning to Colby to become daily visitors to Oney's, but you know kids, especially me! My attention span couldn't handle thinking of college more than six months away. I mean, Christmas was only a couple of weeks away, and I hadn't even thought about that!

My sleeping hours were as strange in 1949 as they are now, so I was up at four or five o'clock on Christmas morning. Complete silence welcomed me to the living room and the Christmas tree. There, resting like the trophy it has become, sat the Colby mug on its own throne! A full case – yes, twenty-four cans of Schlitz beer – was the resting-place for the beer stein.

How did Sister get a case of beer? Where did she get enough money for both the stein and the liquid to fill it? Well, that didn't matter at the moment, because as far as I was concerned, it was appropriate to enjoy "The Breakfast of Champions" – Schlitz!

Opening the note tied to the mug handle said it all, "Jackie, sure was nice of you and Bobby to come all the way to Waterville to see me. You deserve a little bit of Oney's right here on Pleasant Street! Merry Christmas! Sister."

What a gift! – What a memory! – What a sister!

FRIDAY NIGHT MOVIES

To this very day, I can smell the popcorn in the lobby of the Cleveland Circle Movie Theater! I can see the adorable girls on one side of the lobby, and the boys, just like in dancing school, on the other side. It was Friday night at the movies!

I don't remember exactly how it came about, but for many months it went like clockwork. Kids showed up at the flick at the Circle. It didn't matter what was playing. No one cared. It was just a gathering place where you might actually sit next to a girl you knew at school. It wasn't a date. You just arrived and bought your ticket – fifteen cents or so – and the girls did the same. Then you'd get up your nerve and mingle with the girls and if you were lucky, sit with one of them. Some guys were fortunate enough to meet the same girl almost every week, and be by her side when the movie started. I, thankfully, was one of those guys in 1944!

There I sat with Mary, the beautiful girl from dancing school who I had a crush on, but of course, never let on that I did. The lights would dim, and that's when your thoughts about the movie left you. My only goal was to get up the nerve to put my arm around Mary's shoulder. This was a big deal, and took planning.

The movement was slow, very slow, as you snuck your arm up around the back of the plush seat where "Miss Gorgeous" sat. Many minutes later, you held your breath, and actually touched her shoulders! As the flick progressed, you got bolder and put your whole hand on her shoulder, not just a finger or two. After twenty minutes of your arm being in one position, it would start to fall asleep and drive you nuts, but no way would you ever move that arm!

The movie ended, and all the kids ended up in the lobby – girls on one side – boys on the other. When I got home I'd smile from within, knowing that I'd see Mary again next week. Maybe within a month or so I'd get up my courage to hold her hand or maybe tell her how pretty she was. Wow! That would really be something!

THE TOTEM POLE BALLROOM

One of the delights stuck in the back of my Memory Bank is the Totem Pole Ballroom that was in the old Norumbega Park in Auburndale, Massachusetts. "The Pole" was known countrywide as one of the best dance clubs in America. Big bands were the rave at the time – Harry James, Billy May, the Elgart Brothers (Les and Larry), Les Brown, Artie Shaw – you name them and they were at "The Pole."

The Totem Pole was ahead of its time. Tiers of beautifully upholstered built-in couches resting on thick carpeting surrounded the stage and dance floors. You could be on the fourth tier, and the acoustics were so good you'd think you were standing next to the band.

The ultimate way to impress a young lady was to invite her to the Totem Pole. They served no alcohol, and the dress code was very strict. It was an expensive date, which required saving for a number of weeks to go there, but what a great experience it was.

Times change, and many times not for the better as far as many of us are concerned. I guess it was in the 1960s that Norumbega Park and "The Pole" were bulldozed down, and a Marriott Hotel replaced it – ugh!

The other wonderful nightspot was the Meadows in Framingham – dinner, dancing, and an alcoholic beverage, if you looked old enough. I didn't! Live radio broadcasts from the Meadows went out on the airwaves and I'll never forget the announcer with his smooth baritone voice, and gleaming smile – "Ladies and Gentlemen, live from the beautiful Meadows in Framingham, Massachusetts, Vaughn Monroe!"

Vaughn Monroe lived nearby in Newton, but was a worldwide star with a wonderful deep voice. He would croon, "Racing with the Moon," and you'd slow dance around the dance floor as if you were in a movie. Of course you had to double your paper route for a couple of months to pay the tab, but it was well worth it.

Whoever you took would tell all her girlfriends, "Jack Orth took me to the Meadows!" Wonderful public relations for a seventeen-year-old kid, who tried to imitate Fred Astaire or Gene Kelly, but would gladly settle for Arthur Murray!

THE SWIMMING HOLE

Remember reading about Tom Sawyer and Huckleberry Finn? They did a lot of exciting things, but I always remembered their visits to the swimming hole, and in 1940 I was introduced to one by my father. Dover, west of Boston, was considered way out in the country then, and my father would take me to a swimming hole he knew when he was a kid. It even had a heavy rope on a tree that you could swing out over the water and jump in. I loved going there!

Not far from the swimming hole was a sand pit area that was perfect for shooting at targets with my Red Rider BB gun. We'd set up a couple of tin cans and shoot for hours, then head back to the swimming hole.

It's funny the little things you can pull from your Memory Bank. Upon leaving the swimming hole one day, we saw a large turtle crossing a nearby paved road. My Dad immediately stopped the car and went and got the turtle.

"We don't want him to get run over, Jackson. We'll take him to the swimming hole!"

That made a huge impression on me, and that gesture has stuck with me all my life. We put the turtle in the water and off he went towards some pond lilies on the other side. Thinking back I swear that turtle nodded his head in thanks as we placed him in the water!

On the way home, we stopped at Howard Johnson's for one of their twenty-eight flavors of ice cream. Those little withdrawals from one's Memory Bank have gained interest over the years, and are worth millions now.

THE WHITE LIE BACKFIRED

In 1945 or '46, I was at home for a long weekend from school in Derry, New Hampshire. Being a kid who never enjoyed the "schooling" part of school, I wasn't looking forward to attending school on Monday. I casually mentioned in the morning, that I had a bad stomach ache that seemed to be getting a little worse. I figured that would get me a reprieve until at least Monday, and I wouldn't have to go back until late Monday for school on Tuesday.

My mother was worried about having me go back to school if I was getting pains in my stomach, so she called our doctor, who lived only a couple of miles away. His office, like many doctors then, was right at his house. Doctors then, unlike now, made house calls or had you come to their office, even on a Sunday. So off we went to see the doctor.

Doctor Smith (not his real name) asked me about the pain, which of course I didn't have, and I embellished on my previous lie to my parents. He checked me out on the examining table – pushed me here and there asking if that hurt. I, of course, told him it did, which it didn't, when he pushed a certain spot. He consulted with my parents with me on the table listening.

"Mr. and Mrs. Orth, I believe Jack has appendicitis and an appendectomy is probably called for. I suggest we take care of it before he has any major problem."

There I am on the table, without any pain at all – only the pain of telling my parents I was only lying to get out of going to school. My pea brain filtered that information through the cycle that would determine what I would say. My brain worked as fast as today's computers and spit out an instant decision – say nothing! How could I confess to an out and out lie? I couldn't, so off to the hospital I went.

They took out my appendix and I spent at least five days in the hospital in Newton. Then I was kept at home for a week or two before I was allowed to head back to school. I never told my parents, even when they were well on in years, that I had faked the whole deal!

In drawing this memory out of The Bank, I can't help but laugh hysterically when I think of that day at the doctor's office. He was so serious, along with my parents. It never entered my mind to blow the whistle on myself. If I did, my parents would have always questioned my future statements to them, always wondering if I was telling the truth. No, I had to stick to my story and bid farewell to my appendix!

THE BOSTON MARATHON

In the 1930s and 40s, the Boston Marathon had nowhere near the number of runners they have now, but the twenty-six mile route from Hopkinton to Boston was always packed with people cheering them on during the grueling run. It all began in 1897, the first marathon run in the United States, and now over 30,000 runners participate.

Every April on Patriot's Day, we would all gather at Commonwealth Avenue in Newton Center to take in the race. From our vantage point, the finish line was about seven miles away, and our favorite spot to watch was from Chuck Phaneuf's house halfway up the hill before the runners reached the next hill called "Heart Break Hill." The race of 1945 or 1946 was a little different for us than any race we ever went to.

Chuck Phaneuf was a genius with anything mechanical, electrical, or in whatever else he was doing. Chuck would become an engineer, and showed us one of the reasons why on that marathon day. His big brick house halfway up the hill from the Commonwealth/Walnut intersection was the perfect set up. Up on the roof we went, and Chuck had rigged up a loud speaker you could hear a half-mile away! We had binoculars and would scan down the hill toward City Hall, check the number on the runner's shirt, and proceed to announce him before he passed us by.

So, as the runner crossed Walnut Street and headed up the hill, a loud message would be sent through the speaker – "Let's welcome Boston's own, Johnny Kelly. Good luck Johnny!" or "Here comes Tarzan Brown. A big hand for Tarzan Brown!" or "Welcome to Clarence Demar, one of the great ones!" We would continue this for hours and have the greatest time doing it, and just couldn't wait for the next runner to be announced.

Chuck went on to be a Lieutenant in the Marine Corps after getting his degree in engineering at Tufts University. He's retired in Florida, and I saw him last year. We both talked about the many great times we had together that are in our Memory Bank!

A TRIP TO THE OFFICE

Unlike college, there was a real challenge to skipping a class in high school. Skipping an entire day of school was very simple – you just didn't show up! But once you check into your homeroom in the morning, you're there for the day. That is, unless you plan your work and work your plan.

In 1949 and 1950, my great friend Jim Emmert and I worked our plan to perfection, and that caper gave us great satisfaction! Jim had a 1940 maroon Ford convertible with double pipes, skirts, and the customized look that made heads turn as you drove by. The ideal class to skip was the one before lunch, for you then had a couple of hours including lunch break to ride around and have lunch on the road.

We knew each other's class schedule and came up with a unique way of arranging a trip to the office. One of us would ask permission to go to the men's room and go into an empty classroom to call the class where the other guy was. Then, we would ask that Jack Orth or Jim Emmert report to the principal's office. Then when Jim or Jack left to go to the office, we'd go into an empty room and call the other class to have Jack sent to the office. We'd meet at the car parked on Walnut Street and take off to the wonderful rumbling sound of those double pipes.

There was something great about the whole experience! You had the "high" of bucking the establishment – the thrill of putting one over on the enemy – and lunch always tasted better when you were free as a bird!

A few years later, after my three years in the Marine Corps, I entered Boston University. There were many days, I must say, that I walked across Commonwealth Avenue and disappeared down the steps into The Dugout instead of going to class. The Dugout served tap beer that had that musty taste from not cleaning out the lines of the beer keg, but it beat hanging around a history class! Many other veterans attended class at The Dugout, but it didn't give you that wonderful feeling of breaking out of high school and beating the system!

Now, if Jim and I had known about The Dugout, we could have been there in about fifteen minutes. We may have passed for college kids, and had a couple of cold ones. That would have added extra excitement to our trip to the office!

TRADING COMIC BOOKS

When I was about twelve-years-old, trading comic books was part of a kid's life. Many of us had stacks of comic books, and we'd trade back and forth with each other. Also, baseball cards – I had cigar boxes full of baseball cards. Hmm…if I had those baseball cards now, I'd take them to *Antiques Road Show* to get an appraisal for over five million dollars, and I would laugh all the way to the bank next to my Memory Bank. My old friend, David Clough, was a master in collecting *Big Little Books*. They were about four inches by four inches, but were three inches thick. I hope Dave saved some of them.

In the summertime, I slept in a sun porch on the second floor in the back of our house. It was next to my very small bedroom, but I'm not complaining. I was the only kid with a winter home and a summer home all within one house! Behind the sun porch was a huge tree, and well behind the tree was a house on another street where Warner Brown lived. Warner marched to a different drummer, but that surely didn't make him a bad kid.

One morning at about one o'clock, there was a sound outside the screened window on the porch – remember, it's on the second floor.

A low voice said, "Jack, Jack, ya wanna trade some comic books?"

There hung Warner Brown from one of the huge branches on the tree with his paper boy delivery bag over his shoulder half full of comic books. I opened the screen and in came Warner.

The kid always had some *Classic Comics* that he'd trade for Superman, Batman – whatever. *Classic Comics* were beautifully drawn books of stories like *The Last of the Mohicans*, *The Three Musketeers*, *Twenty-Thousand Leagues under the Sea*, etc. They were fascinating because of the drawings, and many a book report at school was done by reading *Classic Comics*. With the trade finished, Warner played Tarzan, and headed back to Jane at the house behind me.

Warner had a stepfather who wasn't a very nice guy. Grumpy didn't have much use for Warner or anyone else. Down a little hill beside their house was their own Victory Garden. The stepfather worked down there often. One day Dave Clough and I heard his wife whistle for him to come up to the house, and he walked up the hill. David and I had a wonderful idea and we put it into action about an hour later.

We hid in the bushes and whistled like his wife did! The stepfather looked up at house and walked up the hill. A few minutes later, he was back in the garden, and twenty minutes later we repeated the whistle and off he went to the house. Within minutes, he was back in the garden and we did the same thing ten minutes later.

He looked around, and Dave and I couldn't hold back our laughter from behind the bushes as the stepfather charged up the hill toward us.

"You little bastards!" he yelled as we took off like rabbits would from the fox. Over the fence we went with feelings of great joy that Warner's stepfather had allowed two kids to whistle such a happy tune!

THE SUPERSTAR

A couple of TV seasons ago, we happened to flick on *Mad Men*, which we had never seen, but it was receiving rave reviews. We watched for five minutes or so, and suddenly I did a double take and yelled to my wife, Sally, "Sally, Mousie is on Mad Men!"

Robert Morse was playing the part of the C.E.O. of Sterling Cooper, an advertising agency in New York. When I knew Robert Morse in Newton, Massachusetts in the '40s, he was known as "Mousie." He was a singer, dancer, comedian, and all-around fun guy to know. He starred in all the drama club plays and musicals at Newton High School in the 1940s! He was destined to make it big on Broadway and in Hollywood, and he did.

My Memory Bank has a number of deposits involving Mousie. However, the times I remember most are when he used to practice his great talents on the trolley car that went from Cleveland Circle to Boston. We'd be on our way to a Red Sox game, and the 15-minute ride to Kenmore Square was plenty of time for Mousie to wow the crowd, including us! He had Danny Kaye's singing and dancing down pat, and would perform up and down the aisle of the trolley car. Passengers would go wild with pleasure, and he would repeat the performance all over again on the way home from the game!

When he graduated from high school, he headed for New York, and I'm sure it wasn't easy to crack the code of success on the Broadway scene. His big break must have been when he had a big part in a Broadway hit called *Take Me Along* with Jackie Gleason as the headliner. It wasn't too long after that when out of the blue along came *How to Succeed in Business without Really Trying*! He had the lead role as the young guy playing office politics and working his way to the top. The hit ran for years, and

Mousie was on the cover of *Time* and received many awards for his performance.

The best thing he ever did on stage was when he played Truman Capote in a one-man show. His performance was a combination of superb divided by magnificent, plus marvelous and wonderful! In other words it was the best, and won him many awards. We went backstage to see him when the show hit Boston before they opened in New York to rave reviews.

It was great to visit with him, and to see a guy who knew exactly what he wanted to do in life when he was a young kid – and went ahead and did it. Robert Morse will always be Mousie to those who knew him in high school, but he was the furthest away from being "mousy" as anyone ever was. It took great dedication, hard work, and a real "go for it" attitude to accomplish what he did. Of course great talent was in the mix!!

I think there should be a Mousie Morse star engraved on the floor of every trolley that rides those tracks from Cleveland Circle to Kenmore Square in Boston!!

THE POCKETBOOK

In the winter of 1946, I had a long weekend off from school in New Hampshire, and headed to Boston on the bus. Then, I took the trolley to Cleveland Circle where my father would pick me up. I jumped off the trolley, and headed across the street to The Sunspot where I'd meet him. Just as I made my move to cross the street, a car flew by and a pocketbook fell out in the middle of the street! The car kept going as I picked up the pocketbook and put it in my small sports bag. Thinking the car would possibly come back, I stayed close to the road, but no one showed up.

I opened the pocketbook and was amazed at the amount of money stashed in it, along with a checkbook and all the other usual stuff from a lady's pocketbook. I told my father what I found and away we went to check it out at home a few miles away.

There were three or four hundred dollars in the pocketbook, along with some made out checks, many blank checks, and a key ring loaded with keys. My father got the phone number from the stuff in the pocketbook and called the number. The lady was in tears when she heard the good news, and she asked if we could possibly meet her at her beauty parlor in Cleveland Circle the next morning – a Saturday. The keys to her shop were in the bag, along with paychecks and cash to deposit in the bank. We met her at the shop.

She hugged me like I was a long lost son, and opened up the shop. When she found out about our family she asked my father to please have my mother and older sister come by for free hairdos for as long as they wished! She gave me $25.00, which I tried to refuse but she wouldn't hear of it. That twenty-five bucks was way more than the Rawlings "Claw" first baseman's mitt I wanted to buy! I bought it with many greenbacks left over.

My father told me that the joy the woman showed for what we did for her was worth more than $25.00. It was something that she and I would always remember. An act of kindness from one person to another can never be measured in dollars he said. I remember that to this day.

Once in awhile my father would smoke a cigar or a pipe. With some of my money left after purchasing the glove, I bought some pipe tobacco and cigars for my father at Garb's Drugs in Newton Center. Anyone under eighteen then had to have a note from parents to buy cigarettes, or any tobacco item. My mother wrote the note for me, and while I was there, I bought her a box of candy.

My twenty-five bucks were gone, but it sure made for a nice memory to take out of The Bank from time to time.

SEE YA AT ART'S

The Narragansett Ale sign, adorned with the imprint Art Carroll's Grill, made the little brick building a historic landmark to many of us in the 1940s and '50s. In later years, *Cheers,* the watering hole in Boston across from the Public Gardens, became famous because each TV episode began with the lyrics – "A place you can go where everyone knows your name."

Well, all of the alumni of Art Carroll's knew damn well the song had been written about the Newton Highlands grill, and some Beacon Hill blueblood stole the lyrics and smuggled them into Boston for later use! The cast of characters at Art's would be as good, or even better, than a sexual experience for Damon Runyon and provide him with fodder for best sellers for years to come!

Many of Runyon's characters honed their personalities and down-to-earth ways at the racetracks and gin mills of the world, and one would never be bored in their presence. When the horses are loaded into the starting gates for their run for the roses, it's always obvious by their actions that each pony has a distinct personality all it's own. Art's Grill had only two starting gates – one for the bar and one for the small restaurant, and every regular who entered the race contributed in a different way to the wonderful soap opera beyond the starting gates!

My first visit to paradise was with my wonderful friend Bill Ripley. I was a senior in high school, and "Ripper" was three or four years older than I was. Bill was a card-carrying member of "The Free Spirits of America."

In fact, if there had been an official group by that name, he surely would have been the president or at least on the Board of Directors. With his incredible good looks and way with words, he could well have given the valedictorian speech at Harvard, and all in attendance would recognize him as the possible future Governor of Massachusetts! However, he was content to have spent a couple of years in Appleby College in Canada, playing hockey and making friends.

When we entered Art's, he had just finished his workday at the New England Concrete pipe yard a mile or so away. Loading concrete blocks and pipe all day has a way of making the Narragansett slogan, "Hi, Neighbor! Have a 'Gansett!" even more appealing than, "Hi, Sweetie! Take off your clothes and stay awhile!" Well, maybe...

There are certain things in your life that are tattooed forever in your Memory Bank. You know what I'm talking about. They're always with you. Now, I'm not a man of the world, but I must tell you that I've had a few pops at who knows how many "top shelf" establishments. However, no one could hold a candle to Art's, especially when, in time, you became a regular. You didn't get a serial number. You didn't wear a nametag. You didn't take a test. It just sort of happened. You were a regular, and that is very high up on my resume of life.

The grand opening for me at Art's was purely show time. First off, you had to blink your eyes a few times. It wasn't pitch black, just sort of twilight. Through that atmosphere came the combination of cigar and cigarette smoke mixed with Italian spaghetti sauce, peppers, onions, and a hint of baking pizza crust! Take three deep breaths...*That's it! Thanks, Ripper! I'm never leaving this place!*

The horseshoe bar sat maybe twenty to twenty-five people, and then it was standing room only. In the center of the horseshoe stood the all-important draft beer taps and booze shelves. Now, we who patronize the pubs know from day one that the so-called "good stuff" sits on the top shelf, and the everyday bar whiskey is within easy reach for the barkeep. Art's was the kind of place where the top shelf bottles had to be dusted off from time to time from lack of use, but Old Thompson, Corby's, Barton's, Seagram's "7" and the likes were dust free. My kind of place…

As I mentioned, I was only seventeen, and if I had entered paradise alone, I may have been served a coke, or nothing. But I was with Ripper, "Ripper, the Regular." As fast as a horse leaves the gate, a draft beer appeared.

"Ripper, how the hell are ya?" said the bartender.

"Carlo, this is my pal, Jack."

The short, slick-haired bartender stabbed his hand across the bar. "Hey, any friend of Ripper's is a friend of mine. Your draft is on me!"

Was I home or what? Then, a chorus of "Hey, Ripper!" a few waves from others, and everyone got down to the business at hand…drinking, smoking, and bull shitting.

An hour later, Carlo was relieved by the night bartender. Butch worked for the City of Newton as a truck driver. A guy from the other side of the bar sent a greeting.

"Hey, Butch. How are things on the trash truck?"

"Screw you and the horse you rode in on. Ripper, next time you deliver pipe to Georgie, drop them on his head!"

The bar broke up, and Butch gave Georgie a free dimey. Yes, I was in heaven! To top off my welcome to the grill, Art himself made his appearance. It was sort of like the first appearance of the leading man as he enters the stage of a Broadway show. There wasn't the applause, but you could sense the excitement in the place.

Art was tall and good-looking, and his casual clothes had the Brooks Brothers look. He could well have passed as the C.E.O of John Hancock, a few miles away in Boston. His almost bashful smile and slight southern accent sure didn't fit the profile of a Boston pub owner, but it was obvious from the welcoming committee that Art was one of the good guys.

Ripper introduced me, and I knew right away that Art wasn't your run-of-the-mill guy. Come to find out he had been an Air Force fighter pilot in World War II who was highly decorated and a Lt. Colonel in the reserve. He flew jets on weekend duty, and ten or so years after I first met him, he became a General and headed up the Air National Guard in New England. Quite a guy, Mr. Carroll, and he also became a friend. So you see, my first visit to Art's was implanted into my memory, never to be removed from the files.

After the war ended in 1945, the troops came home, and the rest, as they say, is history. How Art Carroll ended up in Massachusetts I'm not sure, but he met and married Carlo's daughter and purchased the grill. When his name was added to the establishment it brought good luck Art's way. It was just plain in the cards that the returning veterans would support the oasis. You don't lose often with a full house, and a full house was dealt to Art Carroll on a regular basis.

For one who reaches regular status at Carroll's and other neighborhood bars of that era, it's an opportunity to get a Master's degree in life. I, of course, didn't realize that at the time, but in much later years, when examining my degree from the great institution, I knew my efforts weren't wasted! To rub elbows and raise a glass often with those World War II Era people was a treat, and I'll never forget them.

Danny was no kid when I first met him, but I guess anyone over thirty looked old to a teenager. When Danny trekked all over Europe with the Third Army, I'll bet the younger members of his platoon called him "Pop," but with great respect for his everyday support. He was a decorated combat veteran, not that we ever heard that from him. It was just a known fact.

Like Cliff, the character in *Cheers*, Danny was a mailman. Before the United States entered the war in December of 1941, he walked his neighborhood route, which happened to include Art Carroll's Grill. So, Danny was well-versed in the ways of Mother Nature. Long before stalking the Germans across Europe, he had learned to perform in rain, snow, sleet, and everything else that goes with fickle Boston weather.

When he returned in 1945, he took up the old route again, and no matter what the good Mother sent his way, it never bothered Danny. After delivering mail through a blizzard one February day, he warmed up with a shot of Old Thompson and a draft at the Grill. That little "warmer-upper" package was forty cents at the time, so for a buck or less you could take the chill off real fast.

Butch or Carlo, or perhaps Art, would say, "Tough day, Danny!"

Through his laughter, Danny would throw out a gem or two.

"Hell no! I didn't hear one rifle shot from behind a snowdrift, didn't see one Kraut, and never heard that miserable 'poof' noise that means a mortar round is on the way! Besides, Mrs. Flaherty over on Center Street gave me at least a double of top-shelf stuff to send me off her front porch with a skip in my step!"

Then a regular would repeat the war cry heard so often in paradise, "Have a drink on me, Danny!"

In November of 1950, I joined the Marine Corps for three years. The Korean War had started, and a three-year enlistment seemed like a great idea. Before I left for Parris Island, Danny had a few casual yet sincere words to say to me.

"Jack, when ya get out of The Corps, ya may want to go to college on the G.I. bill. Every Christmas the post office hires part-time help for two or three weeks to help us with the overload. My route will be yours if you want to pick up a few bucks. What the hell, plan on it for Christmas of 1953!"

When you're an eighteen-year-old kid, you don't usually know what the hell you're doing tomorrow let alone in three years! I, of course, told Danny how much I'd appreciate it. Well, ya know how all of us from time to time say things, promise things, plan on things, and promptly forget all about them...well, not Danny.

Over the next three years, I was out of the country for about fourteen months in The Marine Corps, but when in the States I would get back to Boston on occasion. A mandatory visit to the grill was on the top of my "to do" list, and always turned into a hangover of large proportion the next day! Danny never failed to tell me my job on the route was waiting. That's the kind of guy he was.

Just as Danny suggested, I did the route for two Christmas seasons, and I learned a whole lot about the difference one person can make in the hearts and minds of hundreds of other people. Danny knew everyone on the mail route. They were like family. He knew the kids, the cousins, the grandparents, the uncles and aunts, and he knew what was happening in their lives. I was welcomed as Danny's assistant, and treated like a king, as any friend of Danny's would have been. Not only did I deliver their mail, but I delivered their Christmas envelopes and packages back to Danny! Everyone, and I mean *everyone*, had a Christmas gift for him.

I found he had helped them cope with tragedy, sickness, and just plain having the blues. He had helped them celebrate the good times as well. If Danny's mail route had a neighborhood association, he would have been unanimously elected president.

Democrats, Republicans, you name it...the vote would have been unanimous. He helped people. He liked people. He wore his feelings on his sleeve, and all who knew him loved him for it. How lucky I was to cross paths with Danny!

On November 3, 1953, I scanned across San Francisco Bay from the Marine barracks on Treasure Island. Each day for the past few weeks, my eyeballs came to rest on Alcatraz, "The Rock," one of the more famous "slammers" in the world. The long-term guests on The Rock were just that...long-term, but I was leaving Treasure Island and active duty in The Marine Corps.

The last year of the Korean War, although I didn't comprehend it at the time, had done a job on me. I didn't sleep much, and when I did, nightmares of combat situations would awaken me as if I was still on the front line. Heading for the main gate at Treasure Island, I was a bundle of nerves...an accident waiting to happen. All I wanted to do was get back to Boston and see my family. The airport awaited, and ice cold beer was the order of the day for the trip across country to "Beantown"!

Art Carroll himself gave the order, "Jack, don't even take your wallet out of your pocket! You're drinking on the house tonight!"

All the regulars were there. The beer taps flowed like Niagara Falls, and the dust on the top shelf was disturbed on numerous occasions. For a few hours I forgot about The Marine Corps and the Korean War, and just enjoyed being a part of Art's Grill again!

A week or so later, Art asked what I planned to do in civilian life.

"Well, I'm thinking about taking advantage of the G.I. Bill and going to college in September of next year. I was never much of a student, but I'm told that colleges are fairly lenient with a veteran's qualifications for entrance. I'm thinking about U. Mass or Boston University. In the meantime, I'll be looking for a job, Art. I sure can't spend my days on this barstool!"

"A friend of mine, Lee Ricciardelli, flies with me on weekends at Bedford. He's a contractor in Needham, and building new houses in Wellesley. He mentioned that he's looking for a laborer. To tell you the truth, I'm told he's a slave driver, but he can't be as bad as one of those drill instructors at Parris Island! If you want, I'll talk to Lee, and you can get together with him."

In the coming years, I'd have many job interviews, but the setting of Art Carroll's Grill is my all-time favorite! Lee Ricciardelli played the part of a jet pilot to the fullest. He wore his leather flying jacket, the white scarf, and had a flair about him that I immediately liked.

A few beers later, I became Lee's new laborer, and would start the following Monday on a couple of new houses in Wellesley, where Lee would build a half-dozen split ranch-type houses. For the sum of a buck and a half (maybe less) an hour, I was employed!

Early Monday morning, Lee pulled up to the newly framed house in his two-tone Lincoln, and he quickly told me the order of the day was to dig a trench from the house to the street for a water line. Then, he took off.

Even though it was early December, the ground was frozen already. You had to break the cement-hard ground with a pick, and then dig the four-foot deep trench. Lee returned as it was getting dark, and it was easy to see he was shocked that I was almost to the street with the trench!

"I heard that you Marines could perform miracles. Now I know it's true!"

Perhaps the trench was a test, but whatever it was from that day on, Lee and I were friends, and I worked my ass off for him! I also learned how to plant trees and shrubs, build stonewalls, flagstone walks and patios set in cement.

In the weeks ahead, Lee's pickup truck practically became my personal vehicle. I'd make daily trips to Diehl's Lumber in Wellesley for all kinds of construction materials. Lee allowed my wonderful Marine Corps friend, Al Gardetto, and me to use the truck and cement mixer on weekends for projects of our own. The strange thing is that over fifty years later, I still love to mix a few bags of cement in my wheelbarrow and put down a patio or do some cement work in our yard! My time with Lee and his crew was well spent, and I'm sure glad he knew Art Carroll!

Oh, Lee also taught me a little something else about sales. One of the ranch houses was 90% completed. I was sweeping it out, washing the windows, etc., getting it ready for Lee to sell. He happened to be there that day when an older couple pulled up out front. Lee was leaving, but the people asked if they could check out the house. He explained that it wasn't quite ready to show, but welcomed them in anyhow.

The kitchen looked out on a fairly expansive back yard, which ran down to a high cedar fence that just about hid a set of two railroad tracks on the other side.

"I didn't realize the train tracks were in this area," the husband said, as they looked out the back windows.

"Well, we'll be planting a few trees at the end of the yard. There's actually not much train traffic since it's only the commuter line," Lee answered, with his movie-star smile.

The gentleman glanced at his wife, then looked out the window again, and said, "Gosh, I love the sounds of a train and trains in general!"

Lee, not skipping a beat, replied in a very low-key way, "Well, of course, it is the commuter line, so it's fairly busy in the morning and evening but slacks off during the day."

The man gave his wife a look of pure joy. They spent a half-hour or so with Lee and bought the house!

I learned that there is a buyer for everything. A railroad track, or whatever, to one person is an eyesore, to someone else it's a thing of beauty. Never underestimate the value of what you're selling!!

During the last month of the Korean War, I was written up for a combat citation. After being discharged in November of that year, 1953, I forgot all about that, and, of course, went to work for Lee. In the winter of 1954, word came from the Department of the Navy/Marine Corps that a Bronze Star with combat "V" was to be presented to me. Arrangements were made, and I appeared at the Fargo Building in Boston for a short ceremony.

After work two days later, I entered Art's Grill. Four or five copies of my photo and the news story were on the walls of the wonderful hangout in Newton Highlands! I was shocked, as I hadn't seen the newspaper article, and the welcome I received was overwhelming. Endless drinks were served, and each and every person who came through the door came over to shake my hand.

I shall never forget the wonderful characters I knew at Art's Grill, and on September 4, 1954, they once again showed their true colors. Jim Emmert, my lifelong friend, was the best man at my wedding that day, and Jim Waugh, another wonderful friend, was the usher when Sally Fawcett would become Mrs. John Orth at eleven o'clock in the morning. Art Carroll arranged with the two Jims for me to stop by the grill with them at nine-thirty or so for a toast to the day. The place was packed, and Art proposed a toast. Screwdrivers (a drink with vodka and orange juice) weren't seen too often at Art's bar, but on that Saturday morning, everyone drank to happiness for Sally and me!

Art isn't with us in person anymore, and many of the patrons of the wonderful establishment aren't either, but they're with me in spirit to this day. And ya know that toast to Sally and me worked...we've been married fifty-six years!

Here's to you, Art, and all the people who entered the confines of one of the great old watering holes!

THE HARLEY DAVIDSON

Whenever I see a motorcycle, I think of my old friend, Bill Ripley. "Ripper" was four or five years older than me and lived in our neighborhood. He may have been one of the founders of "The Free Spirits of America," for he surely marched to a different drummer, and I loved the route he took through life although it ended when he was young – under thirty.

He was practically a second son to my mother and father, and yes, an older brother to me. Bill had completed a year of college at Appleby College near Toronto, Canada, but was taking time off to travel that different road he marched on. We were all having dinner at my house, and Bill told my parents he was heading up to Appleby for the big spring reunion. He asked if I could go along with him on the motorcycle. I was fourteen or fifteen, and my eyes lit up like the lights on Bill's Harley! But I knew my parents wouldn't let me ride to Canada on a motorcycle.

My mother was the one who would have to be sold on the idea of my sitting on the back of a bike headed for Canada. I knew my father would give a thumbs up on the trip, and I was proven right when he piped up, "You know, Margaret, it might be great for Jack to see Canada and Bill's college. In a few years, he'll be ready for college, and it's a good experience for him."

Without any hesitation, my mother made my day when she said, "Harold, I think you're right!"

The green gem loaded with chrome pulled up to my house early in the morning a few days later. I threw a few things in the saddlebag on the bike, hopped on with Ripper, and off we went. Within fifteen minutes it was pouring rain. I knew if that rain had started twenty minutes earlier there would have been no way my mother would have let me leave.

All the way out to Western Massachusetts the downpour continued. Two guys on a bike in the pouring rain is no fun, but the adventure ahead of me more than made up for the rain. Continuing into New York State was the same story, and we headed north to Buffalo on Route 20.

In a town called Cherry Valley, maybe one hundred miles from the Massachusetts border in the hill country of New York we stayed behind a trailer truck and followed his tail lights so we could see the road – it was raining that hard. Even then, we had to stop somewhere, and Ripper pulled into a tavern in the middle of nowhere in Cherry Valley.

We had soup, we had a hamburger, and we had a couple of beers! Here I was, fourteen, and looking like I'm twelve, having a cold one in Cherry Valley, New York. Life was good!

It rained all across New York State, and just as we got to the Peace Bridge leading to Canada, it stopped. We had driven close to 500 miles in the rain, and it was like the Canadians said, "Hey, it's Ripper and Jack! Stop the rain!" On to Oakville we went, west of Toronto, and one beautiful spot on Lake Ontario.

We stayed with the family of one of Ripper's friends, and the next day drove to the college. The greeting for Bill from dozens of people was as if a rock star had appeared, and they treated me almost the same. Our trip home through sunshine was perfect. We stopped in Cherry Valley and had exactly the same food and a couple of beers. What a trip for a young kid in 1944 or 1945 – one of my favorite deposits in my Memory Bank.

In 1957, my wife Sally and I had two very young boys at the time. We got word that Ripper had rented a small plane up in New Hampshire, crashed it into Mt. Manadnock and took his own life. We were heart broken, as many were, and that day is in my Memory Bank, too. However, the other deposits about Ripper are the ones I draw out of The Bank and send him a salute as I do so.

PINKERTON ACADEMY

In the mid 1940s, I was struggling to get my ninth grade record to the point where I could graduate from Weeks Junior High School in Newton Center, Massachusetts, and move on to high school. Looking back on my school years, I believe I could well have been the "poster child" for ADD! I don't believe they called it Attention Deficit Disorder then, perhaps just "hyperactive" or even "slow learner." Well, whatever it was, I had it!

Over the years, my parents were very friendly with another family from Newton. The wonderful matriarch, and grandmother, "Muzz" Hardy, had grown up in the Derry, New Hampshire area. She had gone to a school there called Pinkerton Academy. They raved about it and thought a small school like Pinkerton might be the answer to my lackadaisical approach to school.

Graduating classes at Newton High School would be in the eight or nine hundred range, and Pinkerton somewhere between seventy-five or one hundred! At least half of the students at Pinkerton were farm kids, and the school offered a course in agriculture that hit my hot button. Never had any class in school interested me, so my parents decided to take a look at Pinkerton.

Derry was about seventy miles from Newton, and in those days was classified as a trip! Today you'd drive seventy miles to go shopping or meet someone for lunch, not so in 1945! Arrangements were made for us to visit Pinkerton and meet with the principal/head master, Mr. Ivan Hackler. The school stood on top of a hill, a two-story, old brick building, and a smaller, white old schoolhouse was nearby. That had been the original school, and was still used for some classes.

Across the road was the school farm. It was a working farm managed by a family who lived on the premises. It was a true farm in that they raised cows, pigs, chickens, and with help from some agriculture students, kept the gem in pristine condition! The farm did it for me. I was actually excited about the possibility of entering school – a new experience for me!

Pinkerton was the public school for the area, and over the years very few students, if any, needed housing to attend school. Mr. Hackler, his wife, and very young daughter lived in a beautiful old farmhouse near the school. It was suggested that I live with them, and I'd have a huge room on the second floor to call my own. The deal was done, and in September of 1945, I entered Pinkerton. It was decided that I would repeat the ninth grade, as my ninth grade performance in Newton wasn't exactly top notch!

My first day at school offered me many "firsts." Most of the kids, my age and even younger, drove to school in Model A Fords, many of which had the rumble seat removed to make it into a pick up truck. You had to be sixteen-years-old in Massachusetts to get a license, but these kids were driving to school. I loved it!

Then I found out right away that I was somewhat of an oddity – a mini-celebrity. I lived near Boston, and most of the kids had never been out of the Derry area. So, within a day or two the word was passed around. The kid from Boston lived with the principal. Be careful! He lives with the principal – he's sleeping with the enemy!

Well, when a few of the guys found out I actually went to Fenway Park to see the Red Sox all summer, that I could sneak a cigarette, or even a beer if at all possible, and knew the same swear words they did, instant friendship was the order of the day. To top everything off, girls seemed to think it was neat to be around a kid from the big city. I hadn't given any great thought to the opposite sex yet, but actually having a number of girls wanting to talk to you isn't a bad beginning!

The farm part of the school, along with the two hours of agriculture each day, was a joy for me. I raised a calf that received a blue ribbon at the school fair, but my pride and joy was the baby pig I raised. She was my project for the year. Mr. Hackler allowed me to keep the pig in a small shed out in the back of the farmhouse, with a wonderful pen for her to relax in. Being a very original thinker, I named her "Pig." Pig became as attached to me as any dog we ever had. There was never a better pig than Pig!

Many a day Mr. Hackler would visit a classroom I was in and announce to the class, and me, "Jack, Pig is out of the pen again. You'd better go and get her!"

My second floor bedroom was in the front of the house and had huge windows. I could practically walk through the window to the roof of the porch without even bending over. It was a couple of miles to the business area of Derry. Many a night I would climb down from the porch roof and head for the bowling alley to see a few of my friends. Our favorite pastime was to go to the bakery where one of the guys worked a couple of hours a night making jelly donuts for the next day. There was nothing better than a half-dozen fresh jelly donuts and a bottle of Ballentine Ale!

One of the many mistakes in my life was not going back to Pinkerton for the rest of high school. After summer vacation, a week before school started, I took off with two friends on an adventure that turned out to be a major mistake. I was gone for three weeks, and I ended up in Winston Salem, North Carolina. My parents didn't know where I was, and when I returned, it was too late to enter Pinkerton for the tenth grade.

I've always regretted what I did to my wonderful parents. Without even thinking, I took off on a so-called adventure with two other guys. They were older than me, and when I look back, it was because I didn't have the gumption to just tell them I didn't want to go! So it was on to Newton High School with a class of about 800 kids – ten times more than Pinkerton. A huge screw-up by me, and a major disappointment to my parents. I guess the moral of the story is, "You never know how good you have it, until you don't have it anymore." I was ashamed of myself for putting my parents through such an ordeal. To this very day, I think often about my mother and father's reaction to my "running away" from home.

They wired me money to get a bus from North Carolina to Boston. I arrived at our house around midnight and came in the back door. My father heard me and came downstairs. I didn't know what to expect, and was surprised at his greeting. With a hug, he told me he was glad I was home and asked if I was hungry.

He fixed me something to eat, sat down with me and said, "Tell me all about your trip. You must have learned a lot!"

I told him I did, and that I hadn't truly wanted to go, and that I was so glad to be home.

I slept out in The Coop, our garage we fixed up into a clubhouse. Early in the morning the door opened and my mother and younger sister, Julie, came in. My mother was really the disciplinarian of our family, and I was afraid of what she would say, so I pretended to be asleep in my cot.

Julie whispered, "He looks good, Mom."

My mother said, "Yes, he does. Let's let him sleep, and we'll make him breakfast later."

My father was right. I did learn a lot. I learned how much my parents loved me, and the way they handled the situation showed that loud and clear. I learned not to be a follower if you didn't want to travel a certain path. I learned that I was one lucky kid to have a family that stood by me at a time when I really needed them to. Yes, I was one lucky kid, and my luck has lasted for almost eighty years!

DON'T LET THE COWS EAT THE GLASS!

In 1947, Jim Emmert and I headed for Derry, New Hampshire in the 1937 Ford "woodie" wagon. I wanted to see my old friends from school at Pinkerton Academy, and Jimmy rode shotgun on the sixty-mile trip. Our first stop in Derry was the diner that served the very best blueberry pie in all of America. Then we went over to the bowling alley to pick up three or four guys from the old days of the previous year.

We all headed to a pond near Londonderry on a winding back road, and I *may* have been going too fast when taking a corner. The wagon hit a soft shoulder just off the paved road, tipped over, went through a barbed wire fence and slid to a stop. There was a farmhouse and barn across the field, and a lady came screaming toward us yelling, "Don't let the cows eat that glass!"

Two windows and the entire windshield were smashed out, and six kids had just climbed out of the wagon. Her main concern at the moment was the cows. As an afterthought, she asked if we were okay!

Surprisingly, no one even had a scratch, let alone any broken bones. My pea brain had a million thoughts flashing through it – none of them good!

The farm lady turned out to be one wonderful woman, and her husband took after her. The wagon was on its side, and the farmer was able to turn it right side up with his tractor. There was a small hole in the canvas/wooden slat roof and some dents, but the old gem was driveable. But no windshield in the late fall made driving like a trip to Alaska in mid-winter!

The farmer and his wife said there was no big problem with fixing the fence, and they didn't even think of calling the police. In today's world, somebody would have sued my father for damages, and claimed that the herd of

Holsteins ate all the glass! I thanked them from the bottom of my heart, and then my pea brain went back to work. How was I ever going to tell my mother and father what happened?

We headed back to one of the kid's houses, and I prepared to call my father. My mother answered the phone, and when I asked to speak to Dad, she said, "What's wrong, Jack? You don't seem to be yourself!"

Well, I wasn't myself and told her I had a slight accident in Derry. I was known to kid about things, so my mother said, "Stop your kidding around, Jack. I'll put your father on!"

The first thing he said when hearing my story was, "Is everyone alright? Was anyone hurt?" When I assured him all was well, he immediately had a plan.

Most families only had one car in those days, and we were one of them. My dad called my great friend, Bobby Gregory and his brother, Tom. The Gregorys would drive my father to Derry to pick us up. Then, they would decide what to do with the car. When they arrived, my father didn't jump all over me, as I probably would have done in his position. He calmly went about solving the problem. I told him I could drive the car home even though the windshield was gone, and we wouldn't have to leave it in Derry.

My father asked Jimmy if he'd rather drive home with Bobby, Tom, and him in the Lincoln Zeyphr or ride home with me. Well, Jimmy knew that with the wind chill of zero, because of no windshield, we'd both look like Nanook of the North when reaching Newton, Massachusetts! However, being the great friend that he was, he stayed at his post, riding shotgun.

What a trip! You talk about cold, but we made it! The wonderful wagon, what was left of it, was traded in for a 1940 or 1941 Ford "woodie" wagon! My father and mother had a talk with me, but not a knock down, drag out fight. It was just another star in my Memory Bank for them – one of thousands next to their names!

The Gregorys and Jimmy Emmert have many stars in The Bank, too. I was a lucky guy to have parents like I had, and friends that stood by me!

Plus, the farmer and his wife have gold stars, too!

THE PASSION PIT

In the mid to late 1940s, the drive-in movies were the thing. They were all over the place in the Boston area. There were a lot of perks involved with getting your driver's license, and at the top of the list could well be the opportunity to graduate from the indoor movie to the outdoor movie. You sort of walked with an extra swagger in your step when you could say, "I'm going to the Passion Pit tonight!" No one cared what the movie was. It could have been *Little Lord Fauntleroy*. For if you had a date with a girl, any girl, you hoped you wouldn't spend any time actually watching the flick!

When you drove into your space at The Pit, you wound down the window and hooked up the speaker, which was attached to the hydrant-like post beside your car, to the window glass, and put the window up. You had what would be surround sound now, but it was crackle sound then. But you didn't care. It was just another reason to turn the sound off completely in hopes of turning into Rudolph Valentino! However, usually your first couple of outings at The Pit you resembled Karl Klutz. You just didn't know the right moves yet, but you would learn, and eventually, perhaps, do justice to Rudolph's reputation!

If, for some strange reason you went to The Pit with only guy friends, two of them would climb in the trunk so you only paid for two. The money saved from the occupants of the trunk helped buy a couple of quarts of Pickwick Ale!

If you needed to make a bathroom call during your stay, you'd notice that well over half the cars at the flick had steamed up windows. That would mean all was going well, and no one was watching *Little Lord Fauntleroy*. If you were unfortunate enough to be in the four-guy car, your windows were as clear as a bell, and you were embarrassed to enter on your return from the men's room!

When the movie was over, the rush for the exit was like getting the green flag at the Indianapolis 500! On two different occasions, I headed for the gate forgetting to take the speaker off the window – once in my father's Dodge – once in his '37 Ford "woodie" wagon. Good-bye windows. If you had been with a girl, it was worth it. With the guys, you wondered why the hell you had gone to the Passion Pit in the first place.

Oh, yes, we did go on double dates now and then. I won't go into any details, but it made for an extremely interesting night. Double steamed windows were the order of the day, and who cared if we lost a window or two? Life was good!

JEFF

We're fortunate that most memories stored in The Bank are from happy-go-lucky times. However, all of us have some that, even though they were from sixty or seventy years ago, still bring a tear to our eyes.

As I draw this memory out of The Bank, sitting in front of me is a brass dog license from the city of Newton, Massachusetts from 1942. For fourteen years, it hung from the collar around the neck of Jeff, our wonderful German shepherd. Our parents picked Jeff up when he was a puppy in Jefferson, New Hampshire. Therefore, they named him Jeff. My two sisters and I hadn't been welcomed into the world yet, but when we were, Jeff became our very closest friend, next to our mother and father.

He never left our side, and everywhere our family went, Jeff was with us. Those of you who have or have had animals, know what I'm talking about. So, I shall never forget the day in 1942 when I came home from school and my father was sitting in the house by himself crying. I had never seen my father cry. When he told me he had just come back from having the veterinarian put Jeff to sleep, the world seemed to stop for me. My father immediately composed himself and tried to help me through this awful time.

Jeff was a true member of our family, and we couldn't possibly get by without him by our side. As the days passed our parents took out pictures of all of us with Jeff, and we talked about all the wonderful times we had with him. It was important that we understand what a great life he had, and that he would always be with us in spirit. Our parents got this message across to us, and in years to come, their thoughts were repeated by us to our children on the sad occasions of putting a family pet to sleep.

In my office hanging on the wall is a large photo of my sister Julie, who was sitting in the grass with her arm around Jeff's neck. The license hangs from his leather collar, the same one that sits in a box on my desk. The memories of Jeff bring a smile to my face, and the photo of Julie with him does the same. In looking at Jeff's license I realize, since a dog's age is figured differently than ours, he lived to be ninety-eight years old.

Our parents were right. He lived a long and wonderful life, and is still an important part of our family. I'm the last living member of the family, and I can still vividly remember Jeff being with us wherever we went. What a wonderful animal he was!

TWENTY-EIGHT FLAVORS

In the mid 1940s, my mother worked at The Boston Five Cent Savings Bank on School Street in Boston. One of her good friends at work mentioned her younger brother, a senior-to-be at Bentley College in Waltham, was going to manage the Howard Johnson's stand at Salisbury Beach for the summer. He and a close friend, who was entering Bentley in the fall, needed a kid to work with them in the summer. Would my parents let me spend the summer at the beach and work at the H.J.'s with them? Well, H.J.'s had the best ice cream this side of the Mississippi, all twenty-eight flavors of it, and what could be bad about dishing out ice cream all day, along with eating as much as we wanted?!

A meeting was arranged with Bill Bartlett, the manager-to-be, and my father and I went over to meet him. He hired me on the spot, for the huge sum of fifty cents an hour, which also included a place to sleep, and my meals at the Howard Johnson stand! Salisbury Beach was about 40 or 50 miles north of Boston. My father drove me up to begin a summer of hard work, serving food at record speed and cooking thousands of hot dogs!

My father was shocked to see our living quarters, a converted chicken coop behind a farm house two or three miles from the beach! There was just about enough room for three cots in the coop, and it wasn't the cleanest accommodations I'd ever stayed in. I knew my father wasn't too pleased with the situation, but he must have figured the experience would add to an overall introduction to what life was all about.

"You'll do just fine, Jackson. Let us know if you need anything." Then he hugged me and headed home.

The stand was a stone's throw away from the beach, and across the street was a mini-amusement park area.

Through the sliding glass serving windows, we looked directly across at the baseball throwing concession stand.

"Hey, step right up! Step right up! Win a watch, a teddy bear, or a doll! Ten cents a throw, three for a quarter! Step right up!"

A guy and his wife from Brooklyn, New York ran the stand for the summer, and they had a fourteen-year-old daughter. Life was good, and the cute little girl loved ice cream.

We opened at ten in the morning and closed up around eight or nine at night. However, we arrived at the stand each morning before eight to set up for the day and stayed after closing time to clean up and prepare for the next day's onslaught of business. My thoughts of "What could be bad about serving ice cream?" were put on hold for a few days until I became what I thought was the fastest short order cook in the state of Massachusetts.

The H.J. stand had a limited menu, which, of course, included the best hot dogs around, French fries, Ipswich fried clams, and ice cream. Each morning, in preparation for the day, we cut little slices in the skins of hundreds of Baldeau hot dogs. The slices helped the dogs brown up perfectly on the huge, hot grill and created an appetizing look. The buttered, toasted roll, also done on the grill, made for a fabulous hot dog roll! I know that for a fact. For each day, I personally ate nine to twelve dogs – a number of frappes, orange freezes, fries, and clams, along with ice cream!

The only thing I had to purchase or chip in on was quarts of Pickwick Ale, called poor man's whiskey in New England because it was a little strong. After a hard day at the stand, an ice-cold quart of Pickwick at the chicken coop was the way to go, and for a young teenage kid, it was paradise!

The wonderful dance hall/night club, The Frolics, was around the corner from the stand, and Francis Langford, the great singer, was the headliner for most of the summer. She had toured the world during the year with the Bob Hope troupe, and was a true star. Serving her an ice-cream cone was a major thrill, and it happened fairly often that summer.

Oh, what I learned that summer! To run the grill, deep-fryer, and cash register with equal speed – to cope with every personality you can think of at the service windows of the stand – to drink a quart of Pickwick Ale real fast so the bottle wouldn't get warm – to actually kiss the girl from Brooklyn on the lips (not like a Frenchman, for I hadn't learned the ways of the world yet), and to get a little something out of each day that made it special!

Oddly enough, I still love hot dogs, and I always slice them gently before cooking. Clams and ice cream are still on my extra favorite list, and you know, I still seek a little something special out of each day as I did at the wonderful Howard Johnson's stand!

There's probably a high-rise where our summer residence, the chicken coop, stood. I hope the people who paid hundreds of thousands of dollars for their condo near the beach have as much fun as I did, but I doubt they will. After all, I stayed on their expensive turf for nothing, drank poor man's whiskey, and ate all the food I wanted "on the house." Plus, I pocketed fifty cents an hour! Life was good!

THE VICTORIAN HOUSE

Jimmy rode shotgun, and we followed my father over to Stoneham, Massachusetts to insulate a beautiful old Victorian house that was built sometime in the late 1800s. Our job was to put a fiberglass blanket on the floor of the attic. The temperature in the attic must have been 120 degrees, and when you're skin is covered with sweat and fiber glass, it feels like someone's sticking pins into you while you're in an oven!

The old homes had nothing like sheet rock or rock lathe for the base of the ceiling and walls. They used inch wide strips of thin wood, and plaster was put on top of it, then painted. When you walked around the attic on the ceiling joists, you had to be sure footed as one slip could send you through the ceiling. We were close to having the job done, but we were probably losing our patience and moving too quickly.

Jimmy fell through the ceiling and nine feet to the floor in a cloud of dust! I got to the scuttle hole in the ceiling and climbed down to find Jimmy covered with white powder and the room a mess. Luckily, the only thing wrong with Jimmy was that he couldn't stop laughing! The lady of the house, of course, heard the crash and appeared in the bedroom in shock.

Thankfully, she was more concerned about Jimmy than the ceiling and was so happy that he was okay, that she didn't even get upset. My father had to get Burt and Bob Langis to come over to rebuild the ceiling and to plaster it. Then, all was well.

When Jim and I look back on that day in the 1940s, we once again realize what a great guy my father was. He didn't explode with anger. He just assured the lady that all would be taken care of, and it was. Bob Langis and Burt Kendrick never let Jimmy and I forget our day in the

Victorian house. When we would put bundles of insulation in the attic of new houses for them to install, the war cry was always heard, "Hey you guys, don't fall through the 'blankety blank' ceiling!"

HANCOCK VILLAGE

Soon after WWII, the John Hancock Insurance Company, with their home office in Boston, built a new apartment complex in West Roxbury called Hancock Village. On the premises of the development was a huge indoor parking garage for the new tenants who would live there. My father had the contract to insulate all the apartment buildings, and hundreds of bags of fiberglass blanket insulation were stored on the second floor of the garage.

Jimmy Emmert and I worked there for a good part of the summer delivering the insulation to all the new units in the development. Truck after truck of insulation had to be brought into the apartments and placed on each floor and in the attic. I was fifteen or sixteen and Jim a year younger. There was a group of painters who were constantly confronting us with taunts that we were putting a union truck driver out of work. Now the painters were the only union guys on the job at the time, and it wasn't mandatory to have a union card to work on the site.

One day we turned the corner from the second floor of the garage and started down the ramp with our insulation. At the bottom of the ramp sat four painters sitting on saw horses having their lunch break. They yelled at us with four letter words thrown in, that we'd have to wait to get by until after lunch.

I glanced at Jimmy and yelled something like – "We're coming down now, so ya better move out of the way!"

They all laughed and continued to eat lunch but changed their minds in a hurry! I floored the car down the ramp, and you never saw four guys in white painter's pants move so fast! Jimmy and I laughed hysterically as we headed for the apartments.

A few minutes later the painters showed up in force and screamed at us as we came out to get more bundles of insulation. My father's foreman, Bob Langis, a Marine from the Iwo Jima campaign in WWII, heard the swearing and came out of the door and confronted the painters. He had a way about him that I loved that said, "Don't fool with me, or you'll regret it!" He used the language of a Marine Corps Drill Instructor, and the four painters melted on the spot, just like I did a few years later at Parris Island boot camp!

They never opened their mouths to us again, and Bob Langis has a spot in my Memory Bank forever for that day at Hancock Village and for a few other episodes. We learned a lot that summer and still laugh to this day about how fast those painters moved their sawhorses!

DEVILED HAM

In the mid 1940s, my father had a small contract to put an aluminum foil vapor barrier on the cement walls of a fairly large steaming room at the Underwood Deviled Ham plant in Watertown, Massachusetts. They received the large hams in burlap bags, and then steamed them before processing them. Canning the mix in those small tin containers is a process they still use to this day. The only time the job could be done was on a Sunday, when the plant was closed and the steam room not in operation.

Jimmy Emmert and I jumped at the chance to make a nice day's pay gluing the heavy foil to the walls. We got there early, and the lone security man let us in where we went to work for most of the day. Before finishing up, we noticed in a canning area that there were thousands of cans of unlabeled deviled ham stacked up to go through a labeling machine.

A light bulb went off in my pea brain, and I figured that a few cans of the ham I loved could be brought home to my mother! We took two or three of the burlap sacks, filled them with cans and stashed them in the wagon. Then, we checked in with the guard and he bid us good bye!

Off we went back home. Jimmy took only a few cans, and I brought the rest into the house and stacked them in the pantry off the kitchen. I wish houses today had pantries – they were great! My mother came into the kitchen and looked with amazement at all the cans. Of course, she asked what they were and where they came from.

In a very casual way, I told her about the Underwood job, and that the watchman said, "Take all you want home to your mother. They're not labeled yet, so it's okay."

I knew in an instant that my mother didn't buy my story, even though I thought I gave an Academy Award performance as an explanation for the gifts!

The next day, Monday, my mother made my lunch to take to school as always. Now, although it's hard to believe, I took four or five sandwiches to school each day! I ate one first thing in the morning at my desk with the lid up so the teacher didn't see me. The others would be eaten during the day, and I never gained a pound!

For months, my mother would make me the same sandwiches every day – deviled ham! I never said a word about it, and neither did she. I ate every sandwich she gave me until the pantry was empty!

The strange thing is that I never tired of Underwood Deviled Ham, and eat it to this very day. That episode took place almost seventy years ago. I figure that I've purchased at least 4,702 cans of Underwood Deviled Ham and more than paid them back for borrowing from them in the 1940s!

There are few things in my life that my mother and I never discussed again after the fact. The ham is qualified to be put in that category!

GEORGE'S CAFÉ

My Memory Bank account has a special safe deposit box in it for stories I remember from my insulating days, working for my father. He, of course, had a crew of guys working, but I was able to get my share of work and so was Jimmy Emmert, even though we were kids. When we put our mind to it, we could insulate a new house as fast as anyone in the business!

During a school vacation, my father asked me if I wanted to help "the boys" on a job. He always called his crew "the boys." I, of course, answered with a "yes" before he even finished his request. I loved working with Bob Langis, Burt Kendrick, and the other guys. It just so happened my first day was on a Friday, and at lunch breaks instead of the guys eating a packed lunch, they took me to George's Café in Newton Corner. I found out later that every Friday, after a long full week, Burt and Bob would take an hour or more for lunch instead of the usual half hour. They would go to a beer joint to chow down. Looking back, I know they really liked my father because they always called him "Orthy," not Harold.

On this given Friday, they said to me, "C'mon, Jack, it's Friday, we always have a couple of beers and lunch, but don't tell Orthy!"

Off we went to George's. The Blue Plate special was 99 cents – a huge bowl of soup of the day and a heaping pot roast plate or whatever. With that came a free dime beer, or a coke. "The boys" ordered the B.P. Special and three beers – one for me! I'm telling ya, the meal was better than a five star restaurant as far as I was concerned. A couple of beers later, we were back on the job.

Well, soon after that I found out my father always knew they took an extra long lunch on Friday, and he didn't care. He told me they deserved it after a long week.

I loved Fridays with the boys, and their lust for life. They just plain enjoyed working hard and playing hard. What fun I had with them!

ECHO BRIDGE

I've never been much for flying. I traveled quite a bit in business over the years but never liked the actual flying part of the trip.

The first flight of my life was with my great friend, Bill Ripley. He was twenty-one or so and had a pilot's license. We drove out to the small Westboro Airport, and climbed aboard the plane Ripper rented. Heading back toward the Boston area, we first followed Route 9 and flew over all the sections of Newton where we lived.

In Newton Lower Falls, the Charles River ran under Echo Bridge. All the kids loved to go down the concrete stairs under the bridge and yell out their name. The echo was incredible. It was as if you were announced in Boston Garden over the loud speaker system. Bill and I flew up and down the Charles River for awhile and then flew lower over Echo Bridge.

"Ya know, Jack, I bet we could fly under that bridge!" Then Ripper took a slow turn back down the river and turned back toward the bridge for a closer look.

"I'm telling ya, Bill, we can't fly under that 'blankety-blank' bridge!" I said with great urgency – or was it panic?

Bill turned the plane back south again, then north toward the bridge. He was only a couple of hundred feet off the ground as he approached the bridge.

Ripper went even lower at bridge level, and we were about 100 yards from the bridge when I repeated my first statement only louder! Ripper very calmly said, "I think you're right." He pulled the stick up, and we climbed enough to miss the bridge!

On our way back to Westboro I asked Bill if he was really going to try and fly under that bridge. He told me if

the plane had been a little smaller we would have! Do you
think that's why I don't like to fly to this very day?

BIG AL

A couple of years ago, I had a book published titled *I Can't Hear You!* Anyone with military experience has heard some drill sergeant scream out, "I can't hear you!" on many occasions in whatever boot camp they may have had the pleasure of attending! However, perhaps that command has never been any louder than at Parris Island, South Carolina in the 1940s and '50s and maybe to this very day.

The two main characters in the book are Jack Harrington and Al "Big Al" Garbetti. They are two young marines serving three years in the Marine Corps, nearly a third of that time in Korea, during the war that ended in July of 1953. The Harrington character is actually me, and Garbetti is actually Al Gardetto. I have written this short story about Big Al Gardetto, just to refresh his memory of a three year period in our lives that was like no other thirty-six month span in our almost 80 years!

Everyone, no matter what age bracket you may fall into, has certain friends that stick out in your mind more than others. I've been very fortunate, and my Memory Bank is filled with many characters like that. I still see a number of them to this day!

There seem to be hundreds of little cubicles in a Memory Bank, and anyone who spent time in the military has a space reserved for just those events. Although Big Al and I both graduated from Newton High School in 1950, and vaguely knew each other, our real friendship began in early 1951!

I arrived at Camp Lejeune, North Carolina in February of '51, and reported for duty with the Sixth Marine Regiment. A month or so later the regiment was headed for Little Creek, Virginia to practice amphibious landings, etc. Well, I had come down with the chicken pox...yeah, chicken pox...a teenage Marine with chicken pox! I spent time in the quarantine area of the base hospital, and when I returned to the regiment they were all in Little Creek.

The Master Sergeant in charge of those not in Little Creek called me into his office.

"Orth, there are twenty or thirty Marines arriving for duty tomorrow. They just got out of Parris Island, and I want you to be in charge of them until they're placed in the regiment when they return from Virginia. Here's the incoming roster. They'll be here by 0600 in the morning at casual company. Get them squared away and ready for duty!"

In scanning down the list of names and home addresses, I was shocked to see the name: Albert J. Gardetto, Newton Center, Massachusetts. Little did I know that this would be the beginning of a sixty year friendship that, and to this day, Al is a great joy in my life! When Al was called into the casual company office to see the P.F.C. that he would actually report to for a couple of days, he, too, was in shock!

At 1700 hours that afternoon, we sat down in the "slop chute" and ordered the first of many bottles of beer. At 25 cents a throw, it seemed like the right thing to do! I proceeded to tell Al about the special S-2 section I was in that soon would be expanded to ten or so Marines. It was sort of a combination of being in Recon Company, being a Commando or Special Forces guy, and an elite group.

The officer in charge of the group was Lt. Peter Kimball, a W.W.II, decorated Marine from Wellesley, Massachusetts, who had been called back to active duty for the Korean War. I also told Al that Lt. Kimball needed two or three more Marines in the section, and I'd talk to him about Al joining us.

I didn't tell him that Lt. Kimball ran our asses off day and night and had us leading night compass marches all over Camp Lejeune! We were known as "Kimball's Marines," and we were known for running everywhere we went! I didn't tell him that either!

Well, within a few days of Al joining our little band of merry Marines, he was ready to kill me! After a grueling four-day field exercise, the 1st Battalion, 6th Marines did a twenty-mile forced march back to the barracks with full packs and, of course, weapons. Lt. Kimball had us run ten of the twenty miles, and he was in front of us all the way. How Al even passed his physical to become a Marine amazed me, as he had the flattest feet known to man!

In the barracks after our little hike, he removed his "boondockers" and his socks and his feet were covered with blood. All he said was, "Why the hell did I ever listen to you?" An hour later, we were in the "slop chute," proud as hell to be in Lt. Kimball's outfit!

Two years later, after we had both served in Korea, Al and I both agreed that we probably wouldn't have survived Korea if we hadn't trained with Lt. Kimball. Many years later Peter Kimball invited Al and me to join him at the Park Plaza Hotel in Boston, where 1,000 Marines would celebrate the Marine Corps birthday on November 10.

Much too soon after that, the great Marine, Peter Kimball, died of cancer. I was honored to be asked to say a few words at his funeral in Hingham, Massachusetts, which was attended by a Marine Color Guard in dress blues. He was one of the great Marines and a wonderful friend. Al and I shall never forget him. How lucky we were to serve with him.

Just before the 1st Battalion went on a five month Mediterranean cruise, Lt. Kimball was discharged from active duty, and Al and I boarded the U.S.S. Cambria in Morehead City, North Carolina. Five months of practice landings, liberty in ports we had, of course, never seen, and getting paid $87.50 per month to do this was one hell of a deal for two kids from Boston or anywhere else for that matter!

We left North Carolina on September 2, and I was seasick for a couple of days. Al was never seasick, not even when the two of us had been transferred over to a destroyer escort in "The Med" and went through a near hurricane! We arrived in Oran, Algeria on September 14 and had one night on the town. What a night it was! Wine, women, and song, and an episode with a beautiful woman in a veil in the back of a cab that we laugh about to this day!

Then, we spent four days on Sardinia, after we had hit the beach for a mock invasion. Then it was on to Naples, our homeport, where we would dock four different times during the cruise. Big Al became known as just that...Big Al by a few lovely ladies in Naples. They always waited for his return!

Our next landing was in Augusta Bay, Sicily. Then, back to Naples and on to France and Malta and two separate landings on the island of Crete. It rained for three days, and sacking out at night in a two-man shelter half is no fun in the rain. To top it off, I received a letter from the girl that I thought was my girlfriend, Barbara Jones !

I go by Jack, but my given name is John, and Barbara sent me a real "Dear John" letter. I opened the letter in our very small tent only to be devastated. I actually had tears in my eyes! Barbara was in college and found someone far more interesting, who was not thousands of miles away...so, it was "goodbye, Jack!"

Al left the tent and must have walked at least a couple of miles in the rain to a small village, and he came back with two bottles of wine that he had gotten somehow!

We proceeded to drink way too much, and I started to really cry then.

Al said something like, "Jack, knock it off! There are all kinds of women in the world. Forget about her, and be thankful you're rid of her. She doesn't deserve you anyhow!"

That's all I needed to hear... case closed. I never thought of Barbara again. We finished the wine and went on with the business of playing war. To this day, I can still see Big Al crawling into our tent with that wine! What a guy!

Back to Naples but before going on liberty, all personnel on the Cambria were warned not to associate in any way with Mr. Lucky Luciano if you saw him. Lucky had been deported back to Italy, as he had been one of the kingpins in Murder, Inc. in Chicago.

Sure enough Luciano's cohorts sent drinks to our table, and we then met the man himself! Al, being Italian, was a big hit with Lucky, and since I was with him, I was considered a good guy, too. What an experience, but you grow to expect things like that when you're with Big Al!

Our most exciting landing was when Al and I were transferred from The Cobb to the submarine, U.S.S. Tigrone in the middle of a storm. Navy frogmen were going to place demolition near the shore of Sicily for extra realism for our second landing there. Al and I were to take a two-man raft off the sub to a nearby island and call in air support.

We lost our small outboard motor, as Al pulled the starter cord too hard, and the mini-motor flew over the bow of the boat! We were in shock, as was our lieutenant and the sub commander in the conning tower! Well, ya had to be there, but take it from me, it was quite a sight!

We rowed to the island and set up camp. During the night we were surrounded by a huge herd of goats, and thought we had screwed up the landing by not calling in the air support! Somehow, the planes came onto the beach on their own, and we were congratulated on a job well done! Over the years, Al and I have embellished on that story and laugh hysterically every time we tell it.

Back to the States in late January of 1952, where we began our almost monthly request for combat duty in Korea. We wrote to Headquarters Marine Corps in DC through our top sergeant at Headquarters Service Company of the 6th Marine Regiment. Why is it that most young Marines, if there is combat anywhere in the world, want to go wherever the action is? Then, of course, once your request is accepted and you get your first real taste of incoming and horror, you wonder what the hell you were thinking!

During our nine-month wait for our Korea duty to actually happen, we continued to train at Lejeune. We both reached the rank of sergeant, and Big Al somehow bought a car! The 1949 Chrysler four-door served us well. It may still hold the speed record from Lejeune to New York City and Boston!

Al's plan was to make the monthly car payments by taking other Marine riders to New York City on weekends. One of us or both would haul three or four Marines to New York for $20 each, round trip. Remember, gas was only 25 cents or so a gallon, and two or three trips a month more than paid for the car!

Many of Al's relatives lived in Tuckahoe, just outside New York City, and we'd stay at Aunt Anna's house. I became "one of the family" and will never forget the kindness from all the aunts and uncles. Oh, and I can't forget about the food! It was like eating at the best Italian restaurants in New York!

The main gate at Camp Lejeune at 4:30 on a Friday afternoon was like the start of the Indianapolis 500, only there were hundreds of cars waiting for the green flag! Route 258 North to Wilson, North Carolina area, then Route 301 into Virginia, and beyond. We'd reach New York in the early morning darkness, drop off the riders in the city, and pick them up at one or two o'clock on Sunday afternoon. What a way to make a buck, but we loved it! In between speeding tickets, outrunning speeding tickets on occasion, and near auto wrecks, we managed to survive.

Our training and requests for combat duty in Korea continued. In October, I got orders to report to Camp Pendleton in California for transfer to Korea. Al and I were shocked and heartbroken. His orders didn't come through! However, on my fourth week of a thirty day leave before heading for Pendleton, Al got his orders. Perhaps we'd still go to Korea on the same draft and ship, and surer than hell we did in December.

I had been at Pendleton about a month and a half when Al arrived. His wonderful mother (a fabulous cook!) had added at least twenty pounds to his 6 foot 2 inch frame over a 30-day leave, but that would disappear in no time from running around the hills of California!

I had met one of the wildest characters in the Marine Corps at the staging camp, where all personnel were waiting transfer to Korea. P.F.C. Ron Forence of Hudson, Massachusetts was the toughest S.O.B. that Al and I ever came across. However, having Ronnie, known as "Flo," as a friend was like having Rocky Marciano as a bodyguard! You were in good hands with Flo! He had been stationed at Pendleton for a couple of years, and knew every drinking establishment in L.A./Hollywood, and the bartenders all knew Flo. He had been in so many fights in various places that he was warned upon entrance on many occasions.

Flo and I, and a couple of other Marines, had bought a 1939 Lincoln Zephyr for fifty bucks from a

Marine who left for Korea before we did. It was in tough shape, but it got us to Hollywood on many a night and weekend. Al's first night in California included a trip to Hollywood, and he saw Flo in action.

Now, Big Al was no slouch in the "taking care of himself" area, but when he saw Flo take off the gloves, he said to me more than once, "Jack, I'm sure glad Flo likes us so much!!"

Ronnie Forence, Flo, died in 2004 in Ft. Meyers, Florida. I visited with him a few months before he died. For three years he had dialysis three times a week, had a leg amputated, and had many other medical problems, but he was the same old Flo – language that would put a longshoreman to shame, a stare that would truly scare the hell out of many, and the same wild lifestyle he had in 1953.

The troop ship brought us to Kobe, Japan and then to Inchon, Korea, and it took about twelve days to get us there. Hundreds of Marines were cramped into sleeping quarters with cot-like bunks stacked five or six high. It was no way to travel, but we found out soon enough that we'd give just about anything to be back on that ship instead of in a bunker or trench line in Korea. We had one night of liberty in Kobe, and believe me there were no holds barred! Flo and Big Al were at their best, and I gave my best effort to try and keep up with them!

There was an eerie feeling in the cold air when we disembarked in Inchon. Two years before, Marines had made the famous amphibious landing there and driven out the North Koreans. Now, it was the distribution depot for everything needed to win a war, including all the troops. Marines were sent to different regiments within the 1st Division. Al and I were hoping to join the same outfit, but knew it probably wouldn't happen, and it didn't. Al went to the 1st Marine Regiment, and I went to the 7th Marine Regiment.

The rickety, freezing cold troop train took us north to a staging area, where trucks took us to our units. Oh, how sad we were to part on that cold day in Korea. Why the hell did we volunteer anyhow? Because we were young, gung-ho, not too bright, and wanted to see what it was all about! Well, we found out, like thousands before us did.

Now, when we watch the nightly news, we cringe at what is going on. Our hearts are with those young Marines as our thoughts flash back to our time under the gun. Perhaps, if the "powers that be" in our country and around the world had all had the experience of deafening incoming surrounding them, with small arms fire mixed in, along with seeing comrades dying every day, there would be no wars. Of course, it would also take a willingness to include honesty, negotiation, and a true caring for your fellow human beings. I'm afraid those traits have been lost along the way.

Al ran a machine gun section in the 1st Marines and was right in the thick of things right up until the war ended. Two weeks before the cease-fire on July 27, I was wounded for the third time, helicoptered to the hospital ship U.S.S. Repose, and then moved to the Naval Hospital in Yokosuka, Japan.

The month of July was one of the worst of the war for Marines on line. The 7th Marines took many casualties, and the 1st Marines entered the picture in the Boulder City, Berlin and East Berlin outpost areas. Al's outfit relieved some of the 7th Marines on line, and he wasn't quite sure if I had survived the ordeal of the outposts.

When I was discharged from the hospital, I went to Kyoto to await transfer back to the States, where I was discharged from the Marine Corps. My weeks in Kyoto were spent in casual company, helping out with orientation for Marines coming there for five days rest and recuperation from Korea. Once again I looked over a roster of arriving Marines, and surer than hell, there in bold print, was SGT. A.J. Gardetto!

We had one hell of a reunion the night Al arrived in Kyoto! Then, the big guy did his thing for a few days and headed back to Korea to train Korean Marines until he was scheduled for discharge to the States.

Al and I had experiences of a lifetime in the Marine Corps – some wonderful, some not so wonderful. Yet we wouldn't have missed it for anything!

As I recall, I picked Big Al up at Logan Airport in Boston in February, and we semi-bar hopped our way over the ten-mile trip to Newton! Over the next few months we mowed lawns, did cement work, and arranged to enter Boston University in September of 1954. College didn't work well for either one of us, and we lasted one year in the academic world.

I was married in 1954, and Al followed three or four years later. We each have four children, and our wonderful wives are still putting up with us to this day. I know they both have been told thousands of times – "You must be a saint to live with that man all these years!"

I believe I have the chicken pox to thank for my long-term run with Big Al, for if I had gone with the troops to Little Creek, I never would have seen that Marine roster of incoming "boots" at Camp Lejeune. Al would have ended up in some other outfit in the 6th Marines, and that would have been a shame.

Oh, what times we had together in the Marine Corps. The Marine section in our Memory Bank is overloaded with data, never to be erased. Big Al is a one-of-a-kind guy, and to hook up with him those many years ago was one of the great happenings of my life.

Our run is far from over. We may have slowed down a little or even a lot, but we intend to keep adding stories to our Memory Bank!

DANCING SCHOOL

Recently, I was flicking the TV remote to different channels and hit on *Dancing with the Stars*. It didn't interest me, so I kept on clicking. Then, I had a flashback to the mid-1940s.

I was thirteen or fourteen years old, and many of the kids in that era went to dancing school. I wanted nothing to do with it, at least I told my friends and my parents I didn't. I was afraid I'd be called a sissy by some of the guys. However, a few of the guys I knew were also sent to dancing school by their parents.

I was sort of a shy kid with girls, and one day a beautiful girl in my eighth grade class said, "Jack, why don't you go to dancing school? You'd probably like it. I go every Friday night!" That was it for me – ballroom dancing and I became acquainted!

The guys were all dressed in blue suits and wore white gloves, and the girls dressed in beautiful dresses and gowns. I always wondered why we had to wear white gloves…I mean, my hands were clean!

The Newton Center Woman's Club was *the* place to be, and there were around 100 kids there. First, we were taught the polite way to ask a girl to dance, and it wasn't –
"Do ya wanna dance?" You walked up to a girl in a beautiful dress, and the boy, dressed in a blue suit and white gloves, would say, "May I please have this dance?"

No close dancing was allowed. Both the girl and boy were practically at attention, and you'd dance about two feet away from each other's face. If you didn't, you'd get a gentle tap on your shoulder, which was the warning to not get so close to Mary Jane! We learned the Foxtrot, the Waltz, and other ballroom dances. As I recall, I used the same dance step for every dance, and it seemed to work okay.

148

The big dance of the night was the lady's choice – each guy would pray for a real good-looking girl to rush over and ask them to dance. One night, the lady's choice dance was also an elimination dance. Each couple was given a number, and every few minutes the music would stop. A number or two would be called out, and if your number was called, you and your partner sat out the rest of the dance.

Could I say, "No"? Of course not, so I smiled and immediately hoped our number would be called first! It wasn't. We went all the way to the end and won the elimination dance. When escorting the girl up to get our little prize, the wedding march played! My friends gave me a hard time for weeks for being married to Miss Unpopular!

There were two other dancing schools nearby – Mrs. Ferguson at the Waban Neighborhood Club and Mrs. Chondroneau at the Longwood Towers in Brookline. They were always short on boys and had called my mother to see if I would show up for "freebie" dance lessons. Now remember, my parents had survived the Depression so free sounded really good! The best part of Mrs. Ferguson's was a bowling alley down in the basement. You could sneak down and roll a few balls before a man named Rolly would appear and drag you back up to the dance floor!

The Longwood Towers was a different game altogether. The ballroom was beautiful, as it was in a very exclusive apartment complex. In fact, some of the girls would arrive in chauffeur-driven cars for their night of dancing.

I shall never forget one beautiful girl who asked me, while we were dancing, where I planned to go to college. Here I was in ninth grade, and she was thinking of college already. I was very bashful at that time when it came to girls, but I figured I'd better bend the truth to impress the girl.

I said something like – "Well, my plans right now are to go to Harvard, and perhaps go to medical school after that!" She was duly impressed and stated she would be attending Radcliff, which was also in Harvard Square. Little did she know that my parents had to practically burn the high school down to get me out of there!

Whenever dancing school pops up from my Memory Bank, it brings a smile to my face. At the time, none of us, the boys that is, would admit to really enjoying it, but we did. There was something wonderful in seeing girls from school dressed so beautifully, and actually paying attention to us, when we would say, "May I have this dance, please?" And then seeing her smile as she said, "Yes, thank you!"

CHESTNUT HILL HOWARD JOHNSON'S

In the 1940s, especially during the WWII years of 1941 to 1945, there were a handful of places where kids just naturally just seemed to congregate. One of those for us was on Route 9 in Chestnut Hill at Howard Johnson's.

Bobby Gregory's brother, Tom, had a driver's license, and many a night he'd pile a half dozen of us in his car and head to HJ's for a great hot dog. One of those evenings I announced to Bobby that Jimmy Emmert and I would meet them there, as I would "borrow" my father's car for an hour or two. I was only fourteen or fifteen, but for some reason my father had taught me how to drive when I was at the ripe old age of thirteen!

During the day, I saw Eleanor DeStefano, who lived down the street and told her of our plan. She decided to join us. It would require her sneaking out of her house at around ten at night to do so, but she was game for that. The plan was in place.

We coasted the '37 Ford "woodie" wagon down the hilly driveway, started the car with as little noise as possible and headed for H.J.'s. There were a lot of kids there, so I was proud to arrive in my own "stolen" car!

After a lot of talk, a frappe, and a hot dog, we were about to leave when I suggested a race on the Hammond Pond Parkway – the "woodie" and the 1939 Lincoln Zephyr! The H.P. Parkway was about 5 miles long and ran fairly straight from Route 9 to Beacon Street in Newton. There were no houses on that stretch of road, and you could get up to high speed before coming to the stop sign on Beacon Street.

Jimmy rode shotgun, and Eleanor sat in the back seat as we headed for our own Indianapolis Speedway. Now, no way could the wagon go as fast as the Lincoln, but I stayed close behind at very high speed. A half-mile or so from Beacon Street, the Zephyr slowed down a little in anticipation of the intersection and stop sign. Well, I figured I could pass Tom and beat him to Beacon Street, and I did. However, when touching the brake, as we neared Beacon Street, nothing happened!

The wagon had mechanical brakes – whatever that meant – and the brake pedal went right to the floor, but we didn't stop! Beacon was a very busy street. We lucked out as we flew across the street directly into a side street in a residential area. A hill helped us slow down, and we managed to pull over to the side of the road where we came to a stop. Bobby and his crew pulled up, and we all laughed like hell except Eleanor. She was speechless!

I pumped the brakes, and for some reason, they took hold and we headed back to the "pit stop" in our driveway on Pleasant Street. Then, I went up the drainpipe to my room!

In early 2000, I saw an old Newton High School directory, listing names and addresses of graduates. I hadn't talked to Eleanor DeStefano since around 1953. I called her up and mentioned the night on Hammond Pond Parkway, but she had no recollection of that night at the racetrack.

Perhaps it was good that she never made that deposit in her Memory Bank!

MARCONI'S

When you're a kid in the age group of fourteen to eighteen or so during the 1940s, you have a tendency to walk off the straight and narrow path of life as often as you can! It's funny how word always got around about what spots in a radius of, let's say, 30 miles of Newton, Massachusetts, would serve you a beer. There were a few locations right in town that would, perhaps, bend the rules, but on occasion you'd need to take a road trip.

Marconi's was one of the wonderful destinations in Framingham. They served pitchers of beer alongside the best pizza in the entire area. You rode out there with great anticipation, and left feeling as though you had climbed Mt. Everest! You felt you had put one over on whoever decided the drinking age! If the great establishment is still there, one may still see hundreds of initials carved in the old tables during those trips by teenagers in the 1940s.

Then, there was Bloody Mary's in Newton Lower Falls. It was a very small bar with maybe a dozen stools and a few tables. If your head could peek over the bar, you could get a "dimey" and a pickled egg for fifteen cents. The beer of the day was Narragansett, who some say came out of the Narragansett Bay in Rhode Island. But their slogan of "Hi Neighbor! Have a Gansett!" made it seem like the right thing to drink.

Pine Oaks was like something out of the wild West! The log cabin style building was out in the boondocks of Natick, Massachusetts. You'd walk in the doors, smell a fire in the fireplace that combined with the odor of stale beer and cigarettes, and you thought you were in heaven! Saint Peter was giving us a preview of what we hoped was where we'd go in about eighty years.

The Oaks had an annual venison stew dinner that would draw hundreds of guys to the party. It was my first taste of venison but not my last. However, the only place I ever chowed down on venison was at Pine Oaks. The stew was great, but after a half dozen beers, anything tastes great!

My great friend, Bob Marchant, and his brother Chico (Frank) spent many hours at Pine Oaks, and one visit really sticks out in my mind. Chico was a gun enthusiast, and handguns were his weapons of choice! The barkeep wasn't too sure if he'd serve Chico, and mentioned that to him. Chico calmly placed his handgun on the bar, and a draft beer suddenly appeared beside it. It was as if we were in Dodge City in 1872!

There were other watering holes we would visit, but my all-time favorite was Art's Grill in Newton Highlands. That's where everyone knew your name, and within a few weeks, you were a lifetime member.

Those were wonderful days. To this very day my favorite places are the out of the way, sort of knock down places that serve good food but not in a fancy way.

Although I enjoy my meals now with a glass of water instead of a few beers, the atmosphere of an old-time gin mill is the place for me!

THE AIR HORNS

In late 1949, my dream was to be a long distance trailer truck driver, driving a Mack or a Kenworth all over America. A very close friend of mine, who was in college, had the same love of trucks as I did. When driving around we'd flash our headlights at trucks to say hello, and if a truck passed us, we'd flick our lights on to let them know it was safe to pull back into the right lane. Once in a while the trailer driver would blast his air horn with a reciprocal hello, and we were ready to join the Teamster's Union.

My truck loving friend, let's call him Charlie to protect the innocent, got the idea that air horns would be a great addition to his 1949 Ford. Charlie didn't want just an ordinary set of air horns. He wanted something that would put us in a class by ourselves. He recruited me, which wasn't that difficult, to head into the North Station and check out the horns on a diesel train engine!

We drove in and spent a few minutes checking out the train yard through the fence. Many of the huge diesels had a set of air horns mounted on top that were three times as long as a trombone, which would make Jack Teagarten envious!

Charlie's plan was simple. We'd simply put on mechanic's one-piece work suits (monkey suits if you will), walk through the North Station to the train yards with our toolboxes, and confiscate the double air horns. With his relaxed style of doing business, Charlie could put the notorious bank robber, Willie Sutton to shame. I must say I was a good assistant as we walked through the North Station as if we owned the place!

The train yard was packed with trains, and workmen, checking here and there, paid no attention to us. The big diesel was equipped with a ladder on the side, and up we went to the top of the engine. Charlie, with the hands of a surgeon, unbolted the horns – one about four feet long, the other about three feet long. I climbed back down first, and he handed me the horns. Just as cool as could be, we walked back through the station with the horns and headed out to Newton!

Charlie was a master craftsman. He attached the horns under the car with the fronts just sticking out under the bumper. He installed a small air tank under the hood and some type of solenoid switch near the steering wheel of the car. The trailer truck was ready to hit the road! We stopped at the Jenny Gas Station, filled the air tank and headed for Route 9 toward Framingham.

The blast from the horns was as if the New York Limited was headed down Route 9! Cars moved immediately into the right hand lane when the horns went off – in unison. Charlie and I screamed out "Whoa!" and laughed hysterically as we headed toward Framingham.

Charlie would pull up to our house on Pleasant Street and give the horns one quick blast to let me know he was there. You could hear the news of his arrival a half-mile away, and my mother always said, "What's wrong with that crazy Charlie Smith, Jack!?"

Charlie became an engineer, but I don't remember what happened to the wonderful diesel horns. I do know one thing. Those horns will never leave my Memory Bank, and neither will Charlie!

THE CRICKET BAT

Next to an antique desk out on our glassed-in porch sits a cricket bat! Sometime in the early 1940s, my father found a really beat up cricket bat tucked away in the corner of a flea-market-type antique store – more junk than antiques he told me. The bat looked like some kid had it and used it to hit stones, for there were scratches and dents all over it.

Some fifteen years later, I refinished the bat, and it sits proudly on the porch shining in the sun. Whenever I glance at it, I have a wonderful flashback, and draw the cricket bat story out of my Memory Bank!

In the mid 1940s, the Newton Center Playground not only had tennis, basketball, baseball, football and a terrific toboggan chute available – it had cricket matches and archery tournaments! I had never seen a cricket match or knew anything about it, but on many a Saturday or Sunday, I would make a great profit selling Coca-Cola at the matches.

There was always quite a crowd at the playground, and the cricket players in their long white trousers and white shirts were the attraction. The games would last for hours, and to this day, I don't understand the rules, but it was great fun to watch them.

I'd pull my red wagon about a quarter of a mile to the Jenney Gas Station and buy Coke (in a glass bottle) for seven cents – then return the bottles and get two cents back – I sold the Coke for ten cents a bottle – 100% profit ain't bad!

I'd take trip after trip to load up on Coke and haul it back to the matches. My wonderful friend Bill Ripley had learned to play cricket in Canada and was invited by the Bahamian team to join them on occasion. He was older than I was, and being a member of the team didn't hurt

Coke sales at all! He'd get the team together on one of their breaks and they, along with many people from the gallery, would buy a Coke.

I recall that my father bought the cricket bat for about twenty-five cents. I don't know what wood was used for the bat, but it looked brand new after my refinishing job. So you see, the cost of a gift means nothing. It's the giving and receiving of the gift that means so much. A twenty-five cent investment by my father has turned into a wonderful reminder of the great days of being a kid way back when a Coca Cola cost five cents, and a cricket bat cost a quarter. I can still see my father plain as day giving me that bat every time I walk out on the porch!

THE AMERICAN PASTIME

While switching through the TV channels, I hit on ESPN, and this Little League World Series was on. The stands were a mob scene of screaming parents, relatives, and kids imitating the Boston Red Sox, or New York Yankee fans when they think the umpire made a bad call against their team. Then the camera zeroed in on a kid who had made an error, or struck out or whatever and he was crying as the coach talked to him. What was going on here?!

Well, my Memory Bank was open for business, and I flashed back in time to the early 1940s. I lived right outside Boston, in Newton Center, and of course the Red Sox were my team. My dream, like every other kid was to play for the Sox in Fenway Park. Well, I spent a lot of time at that gem of a ballpark, sitting in the bleachers rooting for big Ted Williams and crew.

However, I did play first base for our Newton Center playground team of kids around twelve to fourteen-years-old. There were no adults yelling at us, no coach giving us signs to steal, or lay down a bunt – just nine kids playing ball and having a hell of a good time! The only adult involved was a guy named Buck, who would deliver a new baseball to the home team for each game. Then he'd disappear, and we'd play ball – no umpires, no screaming adults, just kids loving every minute of it.

Each week we'd hop on our bikes and head for an away game, or our own playground – West Newton, Newtonville, Auburndale, Upper Falls, Lower falls, etc. When not playing a regular game we'd have pick up games all day long at the great ball field. I may sound like a grumpy old man (and maybe I am), but I'll tell you one thing, I'm glad I grew up when I did. Life was a joy for us. We were more or less on our own, and from morning to night did our thing. Then home for a family dinner, and a radio program. The Lone Ranger, Jack Armstrong, The Shadow, etc.

I'm still in touch with four of the guys from our team. Two live in Florida, one in New Hampshire, and one in Ohio. When we get together we rant and rave about the old days, and are unanimous in our knowledge that we grew up in those wonderful years of 1940 to 1950. They were the best!!

THE BOYS OF SUMMER

There was a wonderful book written a number of years back about the old Brooklyn Dodgers called *The Boys of Summer.* An outstanding array of baseball players romped around Ebbets Field, endearing themselves to Brooklynites in the 1940s.

Diehard fans in the borough of Brooklyn affectionately called their summer heroes "Da Bums." Then the impossible happened. Da Bums moved to Los Angeles! Walter O'Malley, the owner of the Dodgers, who Brooklynites thought walked on water, became a hated man. He was fortunate to skip town before he was found under the water in the East River or Sheepshead Bay!

For a couple of seasons in Newton Center in the early 1940s, our own "Boys of Summer" played the game with just as much enthusiasm as Da Bums! We also knew deep in our hearts that Mr. Yawkey, who owned our beloved Red Sox, would never venture from Fenway Park. Even a rumor of them doing so would surely result in Mr. Yawkey having an unfortunate hunting accident during the off-season at his plantation in South Carolina!

The headline in every newspaper in Boston would be the same:

TOM YAWKEY GOES TO THE BIG DIAMOND IN THE SKY
by Bill Cunningham

While on a hunting trip in his private preserve with members of the Boston City Council, the beloved owner of the Boston Red Sox was accidentally killed by gunfire. The strange thing was that the local coroner found forty-two, thirty caliber rounds in Mr. Yawkey's body. District Attorney James Kelly of Boston, and former Boston attorney Tom Fitzgerald, now Attorney General of South Carolina, determined that the inexperience of the City Council in hunting was the cause of the terrible accident. All twelve council members mistook Tom for a deer!

A local sheriff thought it was odd, since Mr. Yawkey was wearing a Red Sox hat, red warm-up jacket, and red pants. However, it was also determined that all twelve council members are color blind!

Mr. Yawkey will be greatly missed. Jean Yawkey, Tom's wife, will take over operation of the team. She emphatically denies any possibility of the Red Sox leaving Boston, and stakes her life on that statement!

Bill Cunningham – *Boston Herald*

So, with The Sox forever in Boston, life was good! There were a lot of great things about being a kid in the 1940's, and playing baseball with a team of terrific friends was high on the list of summer fun! We had no manager or a coach. The only adult involved was Buck, the recreational guy for the City of Newton. Buck would appear every Friday afternoon with a brand new baseball that he presented to a member of the home team to be used in the Saturday game.

Our home field was the fantastic Newton Center playground, but we'd venture out to away games in Newton Upper Falls, Waban, West Newton, Newton Corner, etc. Transportation was by bicycle, and away we'd go! I don't ever recall anyone getting tired, and I sure don't remember any adult, who thought he was being groomed to manage in the major league, screaming and yelling at us! We were our own managers, and if we made a few errors, which we did, we laughed it off and continued to try our best!

My memory isn't what it used to be, but I remember most of our team. I surely do remember the elation of being on your own with a bunch of kids you loved being with for a Saturday baseball game.

Nothing ever changes in baseball...ya gotta have pitching! Well, we had the smoothest lefty in the business...Bobby Gregory! He had the look of a ball player, and the amazing motion that sometimes looked effortless. However, his pitch would reach the plate twice as fast as you thought it would! Nobody taught Bobby. He was a natural, and our answer to Warren Spahn, the Hall of Famer to be, who was with the Boston Braves. Bobby even had a "pick off" move like Spahn, and we secretly thought the "great one" with the Braves had copied Bobby!

A few years after our Boys of Summer days, Bobby was a top hurler for the championship Newton High School team of the late 40s. I'll always remember his outing on the mound against Waltham, who had the major leaguer to be, Normie Roy, on the hill! The game was away at Waltham, and major league scouts hovered in the stands to check out Roy. What a pitcher's duel it was. Both pitchers were superb, but Bobby shut out the Watch City Wonders one to zip! The scouts left with two prospects in mind, the "Lefty" and big Normie Roy.

Bobby, having many other talents, decided to attend art school at Mass Art. However, instead of becoming another van Gogh, which was surely in the cards for him, he went the route of climbing the ladder to the top in the business world!

At the hot corner down at third base was our answer to the great Jim Taber of the Sox. Donnie "Dunk" Duncklee had a rifle-arm like Jim, and was a vacuum cleaner in the field. Nothing got by him! He wielded a bat that was usually as hot as the corner the field he protected, and Dunk was one of the few that could hit the horsehide into the left field trees at our home field. Dunk was as adept on the ice at Crystal Lake and Bullough's

Pond as he was on the ball field. His slap shot compared with his explosive throws from third in baseball. He became a submariner in the early 1950s, and enjoyed a long career in electronics after his four years in the Navy.

Dickie Farr had the job of calling the signs from behind home plate for Bobby G. It was no easy task to follow Bobby's curve ball and catch the "hummer" that seemed to reach at least 100 miles an hour! Dickie had the bruised fingers and banged up knees of "Birdie" Tebbetts and Hal Wagner of the Sox, and as far as we were concerned, he was right there with them in talent for the game! Dickie went to Nichols Junior College, and his working career was in the industrial field.

Jimmie Emmert played every position on the field, except pitcher or catcher. However, if we asked him to, he could have handled both! He also excelled in basketball, and for some reason, he was as adept at dating pretty girls as he was in athletics! His calling was General Motors Institute, and he later could have been the CEO of the Oldsmobile division of General Motors, but he split for bigger and better things!

David Clough roamed the outfield with the flair of the artist he became in later life. Dave, a sort of jack-of-all-trades, went to Taber Academy in Marion, went into the Air Force, and then graduated from Brown. He was with Dupont, but eventually became a well-known artist with a studio in Maine. He was very talented!

Bobby Kellar could catch, and he spelled Dickie Farr from time to time. He, too, could play just about any position. He went to Moses Brown Prep School, Cornell, and got a Masters at Boston University. He thought about being the next Clarence Darrow, but decided against law school, and went into publishing. School/college books were his bag, and he was an editor for major publishers.

We had Dickie Fisher at shortstop, but I lost touch with him. He was a great guy who went to Governor Dummer Academy and college, I'm sure.

Donnie Hall, another great guy who ran into trouble along the way, was on our team. He was one of the greatest football players I ever saw, but he didn't much care about his talent. Also, he was practically in the genius category in math but got sidetracked in the wrong direction after high school.

Billy Fortune played with us one summer, and then moved to Conncticut. He was a great guy we all missed. I believe Atlee Orr played off and on with us. I lost touch with Atlee, but have a feeling he did well in life. Bobby G's brother, Sonny Gregory, played a lot of pickup games with us, and he would spend hours hitting fly balls with us. Being three or four years older than we were, he wasn't on our team, but Sonny was sure one of us. We had great times with him.

Then, there was Lenny Brown. My seventy-eight-year-old brain kind of draws a blank as to whether Lenny was active with our team. However I think he joined us from time to time.

The last guy on the roster that I won't leave out is me, Jack Orth! Oh, how I loved being part of the team. I saved my money and purchased a new "claw" style first baseman's glove, a Rawlings Ferris Fain autographed mitt that I cherished like the jewel it was. I was a pretty good man with the glove but only a fair hitter. A good curve ball gave me fits, so I'm sure glad I didn't have to play against Bobby G.!

I vividly remember the wonderful field we called our own, the bike trips around the Newtons, and the great friends I grew up with. We were so fortunate to have each other and all the fun times together to salt away in our Memory Banks.

I joined the Marine Corps in 1950, went to Boston University in 1954-1955. As always, school didn't agree with me, so I ventured into the sometimes cruel but always exciting real world. From selling vacuum cleaners to advertising, with a hell of a lot in between, I added many happenings to my Memory Bank, but only a handful are on a par with being with The Boys of Summer!

Wouldn't it be nice to have our own field of dreams? In that wonderful flick, the old time players appear out of the cornfield and romp around the baseball diamond once again. Oh well, we have our own field of dreams in our Memory Bank! Bobby is on the mound, and we're all backing him up with perfect defense. We score a couple of hard earned runs, win the game, hop on our bikes, and ride off joyously down memory lane!

There were many other great friends that inhabited Memory Lane those many years ago. They didn't travel the baseball circuit with us, but were on the "All-Star" list of terrific friends of many of us on the team.

Bill "Ripper" Ripley was a few years older than we were, and hanging around with him brought great joy to those who knew him well. Ripper had movie star looks, to the point where young girls and women alike would do a double take when Bill was in their presence! He had the impeccable manners of an English butler, if the situation called for it.

On the other side of the coin, however, he had the language of a Marine drill instructor at Parris Island, and he could hold his own in any situation that might require any type of force! He was a carpenter, laborer, hospital technician, motorcyclist, pilot, athlete, and surely walked to his own beat during his all too-short life.

I shall never forget the day in November of 1950 when he took me by motorcycle to the Fargo Building in Boston where I was to leave for boot camp at Parris Island,

South Carolina. With tears in his eyes, he hugged me and said, "I wish I was going with you!"

Then, in the late 1950s or perhaps very early 60s, all of us from memory lane heard of his death in New Hampshire. "Ripper" flew a small plane into a hillside, and ended life on his own terms. Oh, how crushed we were. There will always be a spot reserved for Bill in the hearts of many. I, personally, can still see him, and do often, with the incredible smile and wonderful way he had. I'm sure glad I knew Ripper.

Bill's younger brother, Teddy, was his opposite in many ways. Athletics didn't turn him on, and he had a far gentler way about him. Yet, in his own way, he had an adventuresome side tucked away in him that came out many times. One such episode involved him riding a bike, along with me, up to Rockport to see Dave Clough at his summer cottage.

A bike ride from Newton to Rockport was a hell of a long trip, and just wasn't done by thirteen-year-old kids at the time. David's parents were in shock when we bicycled onto their property after hours and hours of fighting traffic on the way to Cape Ann! A call to my parents from Mrs. Clough to announce our safe arrival brought out the disciplinary side of my mother.

"Esther, I'm furious at Jack! We've been worried sick because we didn't know where he was. Please put him on the train back to Boston, along with his bike. If he thinks he's going to have a couple of days of fun with Teddy and Dave, he's misinformed!"

So, back to Boston I went. My father picked me up at North Station with his usual comment. With a sly smile, he would say, "Jackson, sometimes I just don't understand you!"

Teddy went in the Navy, graduated from Bowdoin College in Maine, and enjoyed a long career in sales with

Allied Chemical. He died in Oregon where he lived and worked. I don't believe Teddy was even sixty-years-old when he died. I'll always think of him, especially our exciting, wonderful, exhausting bike ride to Rockport! He was a great friend to all who knew him.

There was Neil Bridges, the gentle giant, who lived across the street from me. As a senior at Peekskill Military Academy, he received a football scholarship to Indiana University. Neil was about 6'3" and weighed in at around 250, and he said he was a midget compared to some of his teammates at I.U.

Neil's father, in his younger days, was the roommate of Jimmie Cagney when they were struggling to make it on the stage and screen. When Jimmie became a major headliner, he was doing a play in Boston and was the featured guest at the Thanksgiving parade. Neil and I went with his father to The Ritz and had lunch with "The Man"! He treated us like royalty, and I was one impressed twelve or thirteen-year-old kid!

Neil died of cancer in his 40s. He had married, and lived down South. I'll always remember him with his deep voice and gentle ways. However, if provoked, Neil was capable of turning into the Hulk, and to be the provoker was not a good idea!

Louie Hurxthal lived in Africa for twenty years. He had his Doctorate in Zoology and wrote many white papers on the study of ostriches. Dr. Hurxthal, his father, a one-time head medical man at the Leahy Clinic, once told me in later years (while enjoying a couple of "health" drinks with me) that "those God-damn ostriches cost me a fortune!" I never told Louie that!

Rupert "Rupie" Amann lived in Louie's house after they moved to West Newton from Newton Center. One of three sons of German parents who spoke with a pronounced German accent, Rupie was the brunt of cruel ribbing during

World War II. I've always regretted not standing up for him in an incident where we, as kids, treated him badly with taunts about being a Nazi. Oh, how cruel we were!

My parents heard of the confrontation, and my father visited the Amann household with me, as I apologized to the Amann family. It was one of the few times in my life that my father told me he was extremely disappointed in me. He then reminded me of his father, and my grandfather, John Orth, who was born in Germany. He painted a scenario for me of walking in someone else's shoes. How would I like it if someone called me or my father or my grandfather a Nazi?

Then, at the Amann's house that day, he told them about his father and about his boyhood in Germany. Rupie, his older brother, Otto, younger brother, Rudy, and their mother and father were obviously impressed by my father's manner and friendly way of healing wounds that could have remained incurable. However, no one was more impressed than I was. I saw my father lay all the cards on the table and speak right from his heart. Oh, what a lesson I learned that day!

I became a good friend of Rupie's and his family, and I learned a lot that day in the 1940s about the horrors of prejudice. My father set me straight on the theme of all people being treated equally, and I never forgot it. Rupie became a professor at Penn State.

Many more memories of the 1940s are lying dormant in my mind. The nice thing about storage retrieval, is that at any given moment, an old memory pops out of the storage vault, and brings you back in time…back to the wonderful days of our youth! Oh, how lucky we were to be born in the 1930s and be able to fill our Memory Banks in the 1940s!

JOY IN NEW ENGLAND

For me, and all true Boston Red Sox diehards, the greatest sports happening to *ever* take place was on October 27, 2004! Winning The World Series of Baseball for the first time since 1918 was the end of the "Curse of the Bambino" for those who had let that media-hyped tale fester and grow within their baseball minds over the years.

But for me, and my wonderful friends from boyhood days at Fenway Park, the so-called "Curse" never really existed or played a part in the ups and downs of our beloved Sox. Now, something far greater than any witchcraft spell has been lifted from the Red Sox nation, and us, by the great 2004 Championship Team!

The mystique of the Yankees was shattered with four victories, after being supposedly down and out by losing the first three games. Winning the last two out of the seven game series in Yankee Stadium will forever erase any references to "choking" against the much hated rivals from the Bronx!

For those of us who basked in the sun shining down on the bleachers at Fenway Park in the summers of the 1940s and treated the Sox like family up to and through October 27, it was jubilation time. After all, when a member of your family succeeds, even in the least little way, you're as proud as can be of them. So, when one of your own climbs to heights considered unreachable, you actually feel the elation as though your name was on the team roster! Family success does that to you.

When watching Fox Sports televise the playoffs and World Series, at first it was annoying to me the number of times they'd zoom in on the fans in the stands. However, slowly but surely, the people watching the game became an important part of the whole happening. The Boston fans at Fenway were in a class by themselves. They were bundled up in preparation for the chill, but their enthusiasm was running extra hot, so the weather was pushed aside, just as the opposition was. The faces in the crowd all had the wonderful determined look of fans who truly believed, and their eruptions of elation and joy were truly a sight to see!

The Team – there aren't enough superlatives to lay on The Team. For me though, it brought back memories of time spent in The Marine Corps. For the first time since 1953, I saw a bunch of guys with an outpouring of a "One for all, all for one" feeling that was typical of a fire team or squad in The Corps those many years ago. The Sox made some errors, left a few men on base, etc., and it meant nothing to the team spirit. You could see it continually when the camera gave us the many close-ups of the dugout. Oh what fun they were having!

When we were kids playing baseball at The Newton Center Playground, we played with great abandon, enthusiasm, and not the greatest skill, but with pure joy. Well, to me, that's exactly what the Sox did, and it was the highlight of my sixty-five years of watching them.

So thanks to the 2004 Red Sox, and yes, to all the other Boston teams who led up to this one. You've all been champions, but the 2004 crew has taken us to heights we've never known!

GO SOX!!!

ALL-STAR GAME

One of my great sports memories is the 1946 All-Star Game at Fenway Park in Boston. The war was over, and all the superstars were back in action. My mother's friend, Charlie Morse, the guard at the Boston Five Cent Savings Bank, supplied me with four tickets for the game. The bleachers, our favorite spot, were the place to be that warm day in July.

The American League jumped out to a lead and increased it to twelve runs to shut out the National League 12-0! Our Red Sox man, Ted Williams, was the star of the show. In his second time up, he hit a tremendous blast over the centerfield wall and over our head about 450 feet from home plate. Then, in the late innings, the superstar knuckleball pitcher, Rip Sewell, came in to pitch in the 7th inning. Rip was the unhittable knuckleball pitcher, but his pitch was called "the blooper ball." No one had ever hit a home run off Rip's "blooper ball."

Ted came to the plate. The third or fourth pitch floated very high in the air and started to drop down over the plate. Ted took a half-step toward the pitcher's mound and hit the highest fly ball we had ever seen. Everyone thought the center fielder would catch it as it headed out to the outfield. The ball ended up in the right center field bullpen for a homerun!

Jim Emmert, Don Duncklee, Bobby Gregory, and I went crazy in the bleachers! We were only fifty or sixty feet from the bullpen and saw history made in 1946 at Fenway Park.

Big Ted went four for four, with two home runs, and we talk about it to this day! There were around 35,000 people at the packed stadium. Over the years, many more thousands have said, "I was at Fenway when Ted hit the homer off the blooper ball!" But – *we* were there for sure!

We were also there for a double header with Cleveland that year. Ted hit three homeruns in the first game, and when he came up to bat in the second game, Lou Boudreau, pulled the first "Williams shift." The second baseman went out to short right center, and the short stop went out to short center field. The third baseman moved over to deep short stop toward second base. The shift worked on his first at bat, but on the second time he lined a deep single to right.

From then on, teams played the shift often on Ted. He could have pushed hits to left field, but that wasn't the guy's style. He just went about his business of being the best hitter in baseball, and no one has taken that position away from him all these years!

How lucky we were to see the great players of the 40s and 50s play. When Joe DiMaggio was paid the unheard sum of $100,000 a year for the Yankees, Tom Yawkey, owner of the Sox, paid Ted $100,001 – a buck more than Joe! Now a player hits 20 home runs, bats .270, and makes 12 million!

Forget about it! I'll take the 40s and 50s any day. It was heaven!

PETE GRAY AND TY LaFOREST

During WWII, a huge number of major league baseball players were serving this country in the military. It looked like our days at beloved Fenway Park would be over until the war was over and the Red Sox players and all others returned. However, many people, including President Roosevelt, felt that the great American game, baseball, was as important for morale at home as it was for the troops overseas. Many minor league players joined forces with the major league players who were still available, and all the ballparks stayed open.

My mother worked at the Boston Five Cent Savings Bank. A security guard there, Charlie Morse, managed a Boston Park League team. The park league wasn't the majors, but there were some great players involved. The short stop on Charlie's team was one of them, and he was called up to the Red Sox to play. Charlie invited me to Fenway to meet Ty and watch the game from a first base box seat with him! Charlie actually took me down into the Sox dugout where I met Ty LaForest. It was a thrill I'll never forget!

A few weeks later, Charlie presented my mother with four bleacher-seat tickets to see a doubleheader with the St. Louis Browns, who, of course, are long gone now. The Browns had brought a one-armed baseball player up from their minor league club, named Pete Gray. Pete played center field, so we had perfect seats to see the only one-armed player in the major leagues and maybe the only one ever.

When the ball was hit to center field, Pete Gray would catch it, flip the ball up in the air, and drop the glove. Then, he would catch the ball and fire it in to the infield. This all happened in a flash and was amazing. His first time at bat he hit a line single to the center field.

My three great friends and I will never forget Pete Gray, and I'll never forget Ty LaForest and surely not Charlie Morse!

LT. PETER KIMBALL, USMC

Most of us can look back on life and pick out two or three people, besides their parents and family that made a real difference in their lives. One such man in my life, and Al Gardetto's life, was Lt. Peter Kimball. He was a decorated Marine, who served in the Pacific during WWII. When he was discharged after the war, the lieutenant stayed in the Marine Corps Reserve.

In 1950, when the Korean War began, many reservists were called back to active duty. Lt. Kimball was married and raising a family, and he found himself and his family back at Camp Lejeune, North Carolina, where he had trained in the early 1940s. I met him there in March of 1951, and Al Gardetto did the same a couple of months later.

I had gotten out of boot camp at Parris Island in late February. I joined "Charlie Company" in the 6th Marines as a PFC. Lt. Kimball was putting together an Intelligence Section of about a dozen Marines to act as scouts and to run recon patrols. This was also considered an elite group at the time. Kimball checked over my boot camp record and I.Q. tests, and I was one of the Marines he interviewed to join his group. It was a volunteer group, and I had been told by other WWII Marines never to volunteer for anything!

It turned out the lieutenant was from Wellesley, Massachusetts, which was only a few miles from where I grew up in Newton. He painted a very rough picture of what was in store for the new S-2 Section and didn't pull any punches. He told me he would run us into the ground, and asked if I was interested. Without hesitation, I was in. There was something about him that told me it was an opportunity to work with a great officer.

A couple of months later, Al Gardetto arrived from boot camp. He was from Newton, Massachusetts, too, which was ironic. I told him about the S-2 Section, and that Lt. Kimball still hadn't found the dozen Marines he wanted. Then, I put him together with the lieutenant, and Al signed on the dotted line!

We were constantly out in the field running all over the boondocks of Camp Lejeune. Night compass marches that we would lead – running through swamps and heavily wooded areas – Lt. Kimball ran us into the ground for sure. However, he was always in the lead and taught us all he knew about trying to stay alive in combat.

At the end of a long day of exhausting work in the "boonies," we were setting up our shelter halves for the night, when out of nowhere on an old dirt road a Studebaker appeared. The lieutenant must have given his wife the co-ordinates on the map, and a dirt road route to get there with a couple of cases of cold beer! He told us he'd see us at 0500 in the morning and took off with his wife! He appeared the next day as if nothing had happened and continued to run us into the ground!

Like all Marines, we'd bitch among ourselves about our commanding officer trying his best to kill us out in the boondocks. But on that night at Camp Lejeune, Lt. Kimball became our hero! A couple of cases of beer and we'd follow that man to the end of the earth and did! Gardetto and I found out when we went to Korea in 1952-1953, that the many things drilled into us by Lt. Kimball could well have saved our lives on many occasions.

Over thirty years later, I had dinner with Peter Kimball and his wife, and I saw him often up until his death around fifteen years ago. At a Marine Corps birthday luncheon in the 1990s, Al and I shared the day with Peter, and to this day, we refer to him as Lt. Kimball. He was the man! We shall never forget him, and what he did for us by pushing us far beyond limits we ever thought possible.

Semper Fi, Lt. Kimball!

THE SPUD LOCKER

"One potato, two potato, three potato, four…" I forget the rest of the rhyme that went with a game kids used to play. I also forget, or never knew, why a potato was also called a "spud," but in January of 1951, another Marine and I prefaced the word potato with every swear word we could come up with!

On the rifle range of Parris Island boot camp, for a week before our instruction in firing the M-1 rifle, two Marines had mess duty preparing potatoes for cooking. I was one of them. The rest of our platoon did mess duty at the huge chow hall, but we occupied a small, stand alone cement blockhouse building called the "spud locker."

However, the wonderful thing about the spud locker was that it was off the beaten path, and we were left alone with our potatoes and cabbage all day. Nobody bothered us. It was an eight or ten hour holiday from our drill instructors each day!

We prepared hundreds of pounds of spuds each day and wheeled them to the mess hall for cooking, along with cabbage prepared for coleslaw. Up until our mess duty assignments we were constantly harassed by drill instructors each hour of the day, so the spud locker turned into a refuge for us.

Very seldom, and not for the first three weeks or so at boot camp, was the smoking lamp lit. When it finally was, five or six drags on a "coffin nail" were all you got! For two lone Marines in the spud locker, the lamp shined brightly all day, as we took turns puffing while the other guy stood sentry duty watching for the enemy! Life was good in the spud locker. I take back all the rotten things I said about the eyes in the potatoes! Cabbage heads ain't bad either!

In 1998, my wife and I ended up in Beaufort, South Carolina. for four years before moving to Florida. I met a Master Sergeant, stationed at Parris Island, who happened to be the Public Affairs Chief there. He was nice enough to arrange for an old Marine to fire the M-16 rifle at the rifle range. Oh, what a thrill for me, and I was ready to re-enlist on the spot! Silhouette targets were set at the 200 and 300-yard markers, and knocking them over made me think I was a kid again.

Then, driving around the area, I realized that just like me, Parris Island wasn't what it used to be! The old wooden barracks and Quonset huts were gone, replaced by a two-story, air-conditioned brick building. Where the wood-framed mess hall once stood was a huge, new modern facility, and the old spud locker must have been designed into the building. I walked around looking for our wonderful little hideaway, but it was nowhere to be found.

Perhaps that was a good thing – who knows? For the first time in over thirty years I may have rushed to buy a pack of Camels and hidden behind the spud locker for a smoke. I, of course, would have "field-stripped" the white gem after a few drags and smiled contentedly knowing I had once again put one over on the drill instructors!!

TRAIN RIDES

In 1939, I was eight-years-old, and my father took me by train to New York City for a couple of days to go to The World's Fair. I fell in love with train travel, mainly because of the club car! I sat and had a great lunch, and gazed out the window at places I had never seen before.

After arriving in New York, I looked up at the ceiling in Grand Central Station. There I saw the painted sky and the stars, and it was one of the wonders of the world, as far as I was concerned! Then, to see the Empire State Building and actually go up to the observation deck, beat anything I was going to see at the World's Fair!

However, the train ride that changed my life in many ways was in November of 1950. I was a very poor student in high school and probably had ADD, but they called it being an overactive kid back then. After high school, I enrolled in Huntington Prep School in Boston to, supposedly, do well for a year and then get into college.

Well, three weeks later, instead of going to school, I walked a couple of miles to the Fargo Building in Boston to join the Marine Corps. The Korean War was on, and that turned into a great excuse for me to leave school and become a Marine. My mother, father, and sisters were shocked! Nevertheless, I boarded a train in South Station in Boston, and headed for New York on November 17, 1950.

With me were a couple of dozen Boston kids who also thought the Marine Corps beat the hell out of going to school. More young Marines-to-be got on the train in Providence, Rhode Island, then in Connecticut. When changing trains at Grand Central a sadness came over me.

As I looked up at the amazing ceiling I had seen 11 years before, I had an altogether different feeling than I did in 1939. I wasn't there with my father. Instead, I was headed to Parris Island for boot camp in South Carolina. Over the years, stories of Parris Island made Devil's Island seem like a country club. Suddenly I realized that the World's Fair was a completely different trip on my beloved train.

The train from New York to D.C., and then on to Yemassee, South Carolina, had a hundred young Marines on board. A World War II Marine veteran of the horrible battle of Iwo Jima worked for my father's contracting company. His advice to me was very simple, and in language I won't use in this Memory Bank story.

"Jackie Boy, just keep your mouth shut! Don't say anything but 'Yes Sir' or 'No Sir.' And don't ever let them think that you're afraid of anything they throw at you! Mind your own business on the train south. Don't play cards and don't drink!"

A big kid from Brooklyn, New York, was the obvious leader of the dozen or so Marines-to-be that got on the train in Manhattan. He was big, loud, and let everyone know that if any drill instructor laid a hand on him, he'd break his neck. Cards were shuffled, pints of booze were opened, and the train headed south. I followed the Boston Marine's advice and minded my own business.

The following night the train pulled into Yemassee. A small, run-down station and a couple of beat up stores were all we could see. The Brooklyn loudmouth opened the train window, and at that moment, a lone Marine appeared quietly in the doorway of the train.

He moved with the speed of a jaguar on the hunt and screamed at Brooklyn – "Who told you to open that window, you maggot?!"

Brooklyn was shocked and speechless as he looked down at the smaller Marine.

The Marine screamed even louder, "I can't hear you, maggot! Who told you to open the window?"

Brooklyn couldn't speak and once again the Marine laid into him. "If you're hard of hearing, maggot, then you can't be in my Marine Corps! Open your filthy mouth and all I ever want to hear you say is, 'Sir, no Sir!' Or 'Sir, yes Sir!' Do you understand me you piece of #@!%?!"

Like a flash, he was at the door of the train and screamed, "Out on the tracks, you #@!% maggots!"

The rush was like people fleeing from a burning building in panic. Then it was on to the cattle car trucks that took us to Parris Island about an hour away. No one talked on the drive to the island. We were greeted in the same manner, and were herded into a long barracks where three Marines continued to put the fear of God in us.

Eventually, we went to sleep for the night, so we thought. An hour or so later, we were shocked out of our sleep and told to fall out on the Company Street.

A drill instructor got our attention real fast, and he told us that they had forgotten to tell us one thing, "Your soul belongs to God, but your ass is ours!"

I looked up at the stars with tears in my eyes, as did everyone else. I'm sure they were all thinking the same thing – "What the hell have I done?"

Twelve weeks later, as we graduated from boot camp, I realized my life had been changed in many ways. Three months before, I was a scared kid who wanted desperately to go home. Now I was going home for a ten-day leave feeling like Superman. I had survived, and I was one proud young Marine!

COLOR BLIND

In February of 1951, the seventy-six young men of Platoon 263 were presented with the Globe & Anchor that United States Marines wear on their uniforms. Somehow, we had survived twelve weeks at Parris Island, South Carolina, boot camp! Marching in drill team unison to the Marine Corps hymn, with total pride running through our veins, meant we were actually full-fledged Marines!

One out of the seventy-six smiling faces was black, although I don't ever remember a colored person/Negro being called black at that time. I also don't remember the Marine's name, but that's no big deal as I only recall perhaps a dozen names of my fellow graduates.

Were we "color blind"? Was the Marine one of us in every sense of being, or did he occupy a separate cubicle in the brotherhood known as The Marine Corps? I don't remember, although I do believe the black Marine lived within the same cubicle as me, as far as I was concerned. Some might say, "Oh yeah, easy for you to say that now." Well, it *is* easy for me to say now because that's just the way it was.

However, if I ever had any doubt about what cubicle a black Marine, or any black person, deserves to live in, I learned for sure in 1953.

Is there any good geographic location to fight a war? "NO, SIR!"

A Marine drill instructor would scream, "I CAN'T HEAR YOU!"

Well, in unison, let everyone who has ever been near a war answer loud and clear – "NO, SIR!"

From June of 1950 to July of 1953, close to two million American military personnel served in and around Korea during the three-year war. Over 35,000 troops were killed, over 100,000 wounded, over 8,000 missing in action, and over 7,000 taken prisoner. So...No, Sir...No, Ma'am, there is no good place to fight a war. I was there, and I know that for a fact!

David "Bee Bop" Harris was, and hopefully still is, a living, black Marine from Chicago. In 1953, he was an eighteen-year-old PFC in my fire team. I was a twenty-one year-old Marine Corporal from Boston. Now, or in a few months, I'll be an eighty-year-old Marine living in Florida with my wife, Sally.

Bee Bop had a great knack for keeping our fire team and squad loose in situations where humor was the last thing on your mind. Through horrendous incoming, dangerous night patrols out in no-man's land, below zero weather, one hundred-degree heat, death and casualties, Bee Bop was as steady as a rock. He wasn't black. He wasn't white. He was just one hell of a Marine, and we all took care of one another no matter what the situation.

When being relieved from the main line of resistance (MLR) by other Marines, and heading back into reserve for a week or two, it felt like you were taken off death row and allowed a new trial! You knew the trial would be over shortly, and you'd once again have to walk the tightrope without a net on the MLR, but no one cared at that moment. You'd get clean clothes, a shower, hot food, and no incoming, and maybe, a couple of hours in Seoul on so-called rest & recuperation!

It was our turn. Bee Bop and I, and ten or so other jarheads, piled into a truck for the long haul to Seoul. The city of Seoul, Korea should have been renamed Shanty Town, for that's what it was in 1953 – shacks, dust, dirt, and a ramshackle building with New York Bar & Grill painted on it! I don't know what the hamburgers were made of. With onions, garlic, and ketchup on them, we could care less, and the Asahi beer in large bottles went down like champagne!

The women…yes, there were women, and for some reason even though we had never met them, they were extremely friendly! I need not go into detail, but Bee Bop and I visited with them a couple of times during our three or four hour stay in heaven. Beer, hamburgers, laughter, and contact with someone other than a Marine. What a day we had! The black kid and the white kid together, but we were both color blind.

Back up to what would be the last mile for many. Over the roar of the trucks, you could hear the sounds of thunder, but the rumbling had nothing to do with the weather. Welcome back to the MLR. and no-man's land! H Company/3rd Battalion/7th Marines was on the move! Also, welcome to monsoon rains and one hundred degree temperatures. It was July, and the sounds of the Fourth were everywhere. If only they were fireworks!

On one of the Berlin outposts, Bee Bop was wounded badly, or "hit" as we all called it. A couple of us and a Navy Corpsman (heroes to all Marines) got him off the outpost. What do you do when your brother is hit? How do you head back to the last mile without him? You just do, that's all. Your other brothers are counting on you, just as you're counting on them.

No way can Luke the Gook end it for Bee Bop! Besides, the lucky bastard's offline! You actually smile inside, as you head back to the squad.

A few days, or maybe a week later, I'm hit for the third time. The greatest Gunny in the Marine Corps, Gunny Parks, somehow gets me aboard a tank, and I end up in a medical tent. Then, strapped onto a cot-like basket on a small bubble of a helicopter, I'm taken to the hospital ship *U.S.S. Repose*. Shrapnel is removed from my leg and back. In a couple of days I'm called one of the "walking wounded," and damn glad of it!

I walk/hobble into a different ward on the wonderful *Repose*, and there lies a sparkling black pearl! I know…I know…I'm color blind, but sparkling black looks so beautiful…it's Bee Bop! Do real Marine's cry? Well, I consider myself a real Marine, and yes…Marines cry!

We went to Yokosuka, Japan on the marvelous, floating hospital ship and into the Naval Hospital there. The U.S. Navy medical people treat Marines like kings, and I know all of us will never forget their kindness and care.

I left the hospital to head back to Treasure Island in San Francisco before Bee Bop did. I know we meant to keep in touch, but didn't, as seems to be the norm as your life moves on. I've thought of him and other great Marines I served with often, and they will remain in my heart forever.

Sally and I were married in 1954, and by 1958 we had three boys. Thankfully, nine years later we had a lovely daughter, and yes, there is a difference in raising a girl! Need I tell you it's not anywhere near as, well, let's just say hectic!

Every Saturday morning I would load the two oldest boys, Jackie and Billy, into their seats with the little steering wheels and head for The First National grocery store. At least Sally would get a little break, and only have Stephen, the youngest son, to contend with for a few hours.

Before shopping, I'd visit a few friends, run by my mother and father's house, and then hit the grocery store. Two boxes of animal crackers were a must, which kept the two little guys busy while we shopped. With the cart half full, I stopped at the meat section for hamburger. All of a sudden, for seemingly no reason at all, Jackie started to cry uncontrollably.

"Jackie! Jackie! What's the matter? What's the matter?"

I bent over to him, and in between sobs I heard, "Daddy! Daddy! That man is black!"

"What?"

"That man is black!"

"It's all right! It's all right!"

Well, in the City of Newton, although only a few miles from Boston, there were very few black residents at that time. Obviously, Jackie had never seen a black person. We all know there are different shades of every color, including white...and this black man was *truly* black!

I turned and saw the man, who was about six-feet-four and could have played pro football. He wasn't smiling!

"Sir, do you have any kids?" I asked.

"Yes, I do," he answered in a very calm, low voice.

In my not so calm voice, I asked, "Did any of your kids cry when they saw their first white guy?"

There was silence, and then a wonderful eruption of laughter from the giant of a man, as he said, "I don't think so!"

Bee Bop Harris flashed through my mind. How I wished he was with me, for he would have been hysterical! We passed the time of day for a few minutes. Jackie stopped crying. The guy and I shook hands goodbye, and as we did, I knew we were both "color blind."

Bee Bop would love that just as much as I did!

JULY 4th

Independence Day, the Fourth of July, was always a great day when you were a kid in Newton Center, Massachusetts. The Newton Center Playground had one of the best fireworks displays anywhere. People would come out of the woodwork on the Fourth to take in the sounds and shooting stars of colors that lit up the wonderful playground.

However, from 1941 to 1945, all was quiet on the Fourth. There were explosions all over the world during those years that had nothing to do with celebration. WWII was in full swing and there were no fireworks. There were no parades. Everyone on the home front was doing their part to win the war. The fireworks were put aside until the war was over.

So, July 4th of 1946 was an extra special day for all of us. In fact, from September of 1945, when the war ended, to July of 1946, there were explosions of joy on a daily basis in support of the troops that had come home, and a place in our hearts for those who didn't return.

It seemed that the fireworks were twice as loud in 1946. There were more colors and shooting stars than ever before. The gem of a playground was packed with many more people, and the sounds of the night were louder than ever. The explosions weren't only from the fireworks, they were also explosions of happiness from everyone. The war was over!

I think back to that Fourth of July with great emotion stirring in my Memory Bank. In late 1952, Al Gardetto and I arrived by ship at the port of Inchon. In Korea, we, and other Marines, boarded a train that reminded us of the old trains you'd see in Western movies, and headed north toward the main line of resistance – the MLR. Leaving the train to board trucks for the final trek to combat, Al and I had sad feelings that we kept to ourselves as we parted company after two years of serving together.

Al would head for the 1st Marine Regiment, and I to the 7th Regiment. Al would run a machine gun section. I would be a squad leader. As the truck headed north you could hear rumbling in the distance, like far away thunder. Those sounds had nothing to do with the weather though, and they got louder as we continued.

I thought back to the Newton Center Playground on July 4th of 1946, when I was a happy-go-lucky kid. I wasn't a kid anymore, and I wasn't at the playground cheering as the explosions turned into a technicolor sky. I was heading toward explosions of a different kind. Those explosions I think about every day, as I do the Marines I served with.

Whenever I hear thunder or fireworks now, it means even more to me than it did that Fourth of July in 1946. Al and I talk often to this day, and realize how lucky we are to be around for another Fourth of July celebration. However, it means much more to us now than it did then.

A SALUTE

Like life itself, the Memory Bank isn't all peaches and cream. Fortunately, the more traumatic or unhappy some memories are, we seem to be able to store them in a separate portion of the vault. This is sort of a "Do Not Disturb" area, not to be tinkered with.

The millions of people who served in the armed services over the years all have a mixed array of memories from those days. Many of mine are triggered, as I know they are for many others, by the nightly news from around the world. The casualty reports from the present war, of course, make all of us cringe, and also go back in time to relive the same experiences.

I don't think a day has ever gone by that I don't have a brief flashback to my three years spent in the U.S. Marine Corps, especially my time in Korea during the last year of the war in 1953. However, the 6:30 nightly news guarantees my Memory Bank flashback isn't as brief as it used to be. When I see the vivid close-up reporting of the medical trauma units, and the helicopters flying out casualties, I see my fellow Marines and the incredible Navy Corpsmen who served with the Marine Corps.

Never have there been braver men than the Navy Corpsmen I served with in Korea. In combat situations under the worst of circumstances, the sounds of "Corpsman! Corpsman!" could be heard through thunderous incoming and small arms fire. Out of nowhere the corpsmen would appear, and with complete disregard for the surroundings or their own lives, take care of wounded Marines. I was one of those Marines on three different occasions, and those corpsmen are forever in my heart and Memory Bank.

As strange as it may seem, and I wonder about it often now, I'd never want to be able to turn back the clock and not have been in Korea. I know, I know. We can't do that anyhow, but if it were possible, I wouldn't because I would never have had the opportunity to be involved with people who did extraordinary and entirely unselfish things for others, knowing full well they could die in the act, as many of them did.

How different that was from the business world and everyday life. Since those days in 1953, like millions of others, I've seen it all… dishonesty, greed, prejudice, and everything else in between. However, I've never seen people literally put their life on the line for others on a regular basis like I did in the Marine Corps.

Our men and women serving in the military today see, and are involved in, horrendous happenings. They, too, will have a Memory Bank filled with courageous acts. It's a great shame that the most honorable memories many will carry with them forever are from a war, but the chances are great that they'll never meet people again like they're serving with in the armed forces today.

Hopefully, very soon the nightly news won't have wars to report on, and never will have any again. In the meantime, all of us may not be saluting those who try and dazzle us with double talk, but I know every American stands at attention to salute our troops.

CALL TO COLORS

I've been fortunate enough to see and play, a few of the great golf courses in America...Pine Valley, Oakmont, Jupiter Hills, Salem C.C, The Country Club, Bay Hill, etc. The quality of my game doesn't come close to fitting their prestigious fairways, but every golf course has seen its share of "hackers," so I don't apologize for entering the grounds of greatness on occasion!

Will Rogers said, "I never met a man I didn't like." Most golfers say, "I've never played a golf course I didn't like." Perhaps, it's because no matter where you tee it up, there's that certain something about a golf course that puts a little extra saunter in your step and a feeling of freedom from the ordinary for a few hours.

Well, if you're ever fortunate enough to play Windy Harbor Golf Club on the Mayport Naval Base in Florida, you'll have a golfing awakening that only a handful of courses in America can offer. The clubhouse isn't one of those architectural gems where you think you're entering the Waldorf Astoria or the Ritz. You're there to play golf, not make a presentation to the United Nations! What's with all these monstrosity clubhouses anyhow?! Don't ya sometimes feel you have to speak in a whisper at some of those country club courses … you know, like when you are in a library? No fun, no fun!

The pro shop at Windy Harbor, and everyone who runs it, welcomes you as a friend. You can pay the green fees, get a dozen balls, a beautiful golf shirt, a hat, and you won't have to make monthly payments to Master Card to cover the tab. Then, when you finish the round, you'll find that no club in America serves a colder can of beer that can then be poured into a frozen mug. Heaven!

Okay, to truly enjoy the complete package and to realize the uniqueness of the golf course, get yourself a

7:04 tee time. Hey! Get up early! You can nap in the afternoon! You'll see wild rabbits, all types of herons, and other wildlife. Perhaps, on the second or third hole, you'll hear a sound familiar to many...the "POP-POP-POP" of a pistol range. Those who have had military experience, especially combat memories, will flashback in time to noises familiar to them, but somehow, not in a bad way. It will once again remind you of some of the great ones who weren't as lucky as you were... and are.

A few minutes before eight o'clock, you'll hear a bugle call echoing over the course...the call to colors. Five minutes or so later, everything comes to a halt. The golf course and the base stands at attention. The Star Spangled Banner, our national anthem, is played. That shivery feeling runs through your body, and it seems like a thousand thoughts rush through your mind in two minutes or so.

You have to say to yourself, "Oh, how lucky I am to be where I am and to live in America!"

If you played every day of the year at Windy Harbor, you'd never tire of the golf course and what it has to offer. It brings back memories, puts a smile on your face, and reminds you once again of how lucky you are. The Pine Valleys and Pebble Beaches of the world don't come close to doing that!

ON THE ROAD AGAIN

In 1982, William Least Heat Moon's book, *Blue Highways – a Journey into America,* was published by Atlantic-Little Brown Books. It was Moon's first published works, and Robert Penn Warren reported it as a masterpiece. He also went on to say that *Blue Highways* is a unique and magnificent tour of America, with the price of gasoline no object!

Well, in our world of 2005, with gas over three bucks a gallon, traveling the blue highways will put a major dent in anyone's travel expenses. Nevertheless, the blue highways beckon, so buckle up your seat belt, fill up the tank, and...Ladies and Gentlemen...start your engines!

On the old road maps of America, the main routes were red and the back roads blue. Moon hit the blue roads and circled the United States – from Liberty Bond, Washington; Depoe Bay, Oregon; Hat Creek, California; Cedar Breaks, Utah; Hachita, New Mexico; Dime Box, Texas; St. Martinville, Louisiana; Conyers, Georgia; Ninety Six, South Carolina; Nameless, Tennessee; Wanchese, North Carolina; Othello, New Jersey; Cape Porpoise, Maine; Harbor Beach, Michigan; Bagley, Minnesota to Shelby, Montana! In between this route, he wound up in hundreds of wonderfully named other towns along the blue roads of America!

Well, over the years, I've hit my share of blue roads, but sadly, nowhere near the number that Moon did. However, on Sunday, October 9, 2005, a roundtrip, a 350-mile haul took me from the red road Route 10 to a couple of blue roads into Quincy, Florida. Being a Boston guy, I'm very familiar with Quincy, Massachusetts, named for John Quincy Adams and his family, but I must say, with no animosity toward the Chamber of Commerce of Quincy, Massachusetts, that Quincy, Florida has you beat!

So, if you wish, and I hope you do, close your eyes and listen to what I think is a unique story of a beautiful little town in Florida that I must visit again. However, I will never again ask for a Diet Pepsi at the Golf Club of Quincy!

When the rubber hits the road on Route 10 in Jacksonville, Florida, you can travel west to California without leaving that red highway. My short haul from J'ville to Exit 181 is just about halfway to Pensacola. My great old friend, Clipper McMahon, left Pensacola and drove east to meet me at The Golf Club of Quincy.

Clipper asked, a week or so before our 10:07 tee time, "How the hell did you find out about a golf course in Quincy?"

Well, he had suggested meeting halfway for golf and lunch, and our usual line of B.S. at the 19th hole. I reminded him that when one Marine suggests a great idea for a day of liberty, the other Marine always carries out the order to zero in on the target immediately!

A fast call to the only motel listed by AAA in Midway, Florida was the key.

"No, there isn't a golf course in Midway, but a little further west there was a course in Quincy," the lovely lady reported.

A call to the Quincy police completed the mission, as the officer reported, "Yes, sir. There's one golf course in town. I don't play golf, but I hear it's a nice course!"

Well, I don't know the woman's name who answered the phone, but when she said, The Golf Club of Quincy, I figured her name must be Wilma Wonderful or Polly Pleasant or some other handle that fits a woman with instant friendship in her manner! I love a Boston accent, and I sure have one, but I may take Southern lessons soon, as she sure sounded good.

"You take Exit 181...turn right on 267...cross 90...past the CVS store about three or four miles...and you'll see our club!"

Is it Sunday yet? I thought. *I can't wait to get on the road!*

The ride from the CVS store to the golf club is something else! Charming homes set back on a country road that reminded me of New England...beautiful trees, hills, and an oasis lay about three miles down the lovely road. I knew right away that this was *the place* – there was (and is) something wonderful about this golf club.

I'm a hacker at the game and shoot between 87 and 95 from the gold senior tees...5,400 yards and under is the magic number for me. However, for some strange reason, I've been allowed to play Pine Valley and Oakmount on numerous occasions...Kittansett, Salem C.C., Bay Hill, Jupiter Hills, etc., etc. But there is a certain something that they don't have that Quincy G.C. does.

Perhaps, it's like traveling the blue roads. You meet the real people of the world and see the wonders of America away from all the glitz and glitter that somehow takes away from the joy of simplicity. Hmmm...oh well, you know what I'm talking about, or you wouldn't be on this trip with me, right?!

As usual, I was two hours early for our tee time, for I'm always ahead of schedule. This is due to a combination of definite itch to get on the road, high speed driving on the red roads, and perhaps, a little ADD or hyperactivity as it was called back in the 1930s and 40s.

I was greeted by a real nice guy in the pro shop who, when he saw my golf shirt with Parris Island Golf Club and a Marine Corps emblem on it said, "I was there. When were you there?"

"In 1950," I said.

He replied, "1954...Semper Fi!"

I know there are certain organizations and colleges that members or graduates of maintain a certain camaraderie over time. However, I've found over the years that there is no "brotherhood" to match the United States Marine Corps! I won't go into detail and incriminate myself, but I'd need an adding machine to keep track of the number of times being in the Marine Corps has helped me through some trying times!

Well, Dwayne, the Marine, and former West Virginia state trooper and Florida lawman, and I had an instant kinship. What a pleasure it was to talk to him. Come to find out, the little town of Quincy (about 9,000 people) had, at one time, more millionaires per capita than, perhaps, any town in our country.

It seems that in the early 1900s and into the 1920s and beyond, Coca-Cola was on the mind of many local citizens…and not just to drink! One of their own had joined the company in the sales field, and spread the word that the product was going to grow in leaps and bounds for years to come.

"Whatever you can scrape together, invest in Coca-Cola stock!"

Well, scrape they did. Over the years with Coke going world wide, and every soda fountain, corner store, and grocery store pushing Coke, the stock split more times than you could keep track of, and a number of Quincy people hit the jackpot big time! It is said that one lady in town (I won't call her old or senior because I happen to fit both categories), ended up with a million shares!

Rumor has it that she decided to sell her nest egg at some time when Coke was at one hundred bucks a share. I once failed math in school, actually more than once, but even my "mathless" mind can figure what the lovely lady laughed all the way to the vault with!

In my teen years in the 40s, Coke was advertised as "The pause that refreshes." The lady from Quincy changed that slogan to "The pause that brings joy to your heart!" Well, at least that was the slogan in Quincy, Florida.

Clipper and I loved the front nine and headed for the tenth tee. By the way, he and Dwayne had been in boot camp at P.I. in 1954 at the same time! Yeah, I know, small world. Rebecca, the extremely attractive/great personality operator of the refreshment cart, pulled up and we got a cold drink.

My request of, "Do ya have Diet Pepsi?" was worse than asking the owner of a new SL500 Mercedes convertible how they liked their used five year old Honda Civic!

With a look of shock, Rebecca, recovering quickly, smiled and said, "Pepsi is nowhere to be found at the club or, perhaps, anywhere in Quincy!"

I, too, recovered quickly, and knowing I screwed up, smiled my best smile and asked, "By chance, do you have a Diet Coke?"

There is an old saying – "You don't bite the hand that feeds you," and I don't blame anyone in Quincy for looking down on non-Coke imbibers!

Rebecca also related a fascinating tale to us that was passed down over the years, and hopefully, it isn't local folklore blown out of proportion. Please, let's say it's not, for it makes this short trip on the blue roads just a little more pleasant. So, I believe that it's gospel!

In the 1920s or so, the local bank that catered to the area was as lenient as possible with personal loans for local residents. Those were tough years with the Depression on the way, and when loans were granted, the bank, as incentive, offered a bonus to any borrower who paid off the note on time. A certain portion of the interest was paid back to them in Coca-Cola stock!

In those days, a loan of a few hundred dollars was quite a bit of money. However, only a very small rebate in Coke stock could eventually turn into a small or even large, fortune. I hope it happened that way, and think it did!

We topped off our day with two super-thick, fabulous hot dogs, French fries, and a couple of Cokes at the wonderful bar in the club. This was a bar wide enough to serve a full-course Thanksgiving dinner on, not one of those little, mahogany bars at some Four Star watering hole, where there's not enough room to eat your overdone burger that costs you fourteen bucks! That is, if they'll even let you *eat* at the bar!

We said goodbye to Rebecca and Corey at the bar, and, of course, the salty Marine, Dwayne, in the pro shop. I know Clipper and I will return when he is once again in Pensacola, or heads to J'ville from Boston. After all, wouldn't you drive 350 miles for great hot dogs, great golf, great people, and a story that makes you so glad you left the red highway and headed for the blue roads?!

I'm sure glad you decided to travel with me. I promise next time I won't talk so much. Well, *maybe* I won't! Thanks for being with me.

HOW I MET MY WIFE

In every man's Memory Bank there has to be a special slot containing the story of how you met your wife. If I do say so myself, meeting Sally Fawcett, my wife to be, could be included in a love story starring Matt Damon and Julia Roberts. Now, I wasn't as good looking as Damon, but Sally could surely compete with Julia Roberts.

Sally's parents rented a cottage on Cape Cod every summer for two weeks, and she invited Judy, a close friend, down for a few days. Judy and I had gone out a number of times, and when I went to Korea in 1952, she wrote me letters. While on the Cape, Judy wrote me a note, and Sally added a P.S. – "Jack, we both graduated in the class of 1950 at Newton High School, but don't know each other. I just want to wish you well. Take care of yourself."

Now, the high school graduated a class of over 800 kids, so no one knew everyone. When I got the letter it was so nice to read that P.S.

About a year later, I was discharged from the Marine Corps and came home. The state of Massachusetts gave a $300.00 bonus to all Korean War Veterans. That was a lot of money, since I was making about 100 bucks a month in the Marine Corps! I put a down payment on a 1951 Mercury. A few days later, I came out of the house in the morning and there was a note on the windshield from Judy.

She wrote something like, "You haven't called me, let's get together." Then there was a P.S. from Sally, "So glad you got home safely!"

I once again thought how nice this was. In a few days, I called Sally, and we talked for about twenty minutes. I must have asked her at least three different times if we could go out for pizza and beer. Sally said she'd feel funny doing that because of Judy. I explained that I just wanted to thank her for the nice gesture on both notes and she said okay.

When I walked up to her front door and rang the bell I was a little nervous, but when the door opened I forgot all about being nervous and just stared at the adorable black-haired girl in a blue dress with a black belt! I wanted to say, "You are the cutest girl I've ever seen!" but I just smiled, and she invited me in to meet her parents.

We went to a nice little restaurant in Newtonville called The Dell. We had a few beers and pizza and talked for a couple of hours. You may think this is corny, but it was love at first sight for me. When I drove her home, I asked if she'd go out again the next night. When Sally said yes, that was it for me!

Eight months later we were married, and we've been married for fifty-seven years. Two brief post scripts on notes did the trick for me. What were the odds of that happening? Sure worked out well for us!

I LOVE THE TEACHER

At some time or other, most young boys, and probably girls too, fall in love with one of their teachers. When I was in eighth and ninth grade in junior high school, there was a female teacher who taught English who was extremely good-looking. Let's just say her name was "Miss Doe" so we don't get into any trouble. Every boy in the school had a secret yearning for her. In fact, it wasn't a secret at all for most of us – all the guys I knew loved Miss Doe! We were fourteen, or so, which would have meant she was at least ten years older than we were.

We went on to high school, but I never fell in love with any teacher there. As I recall, once in awhile Miss Doe's name would come up in our conversation about certain girls in high school – like, "Yeah, Mary Jane is good-looking, but she ain't Miss Doe!"

The next eight or ten years went by, and I was about to enter Boston University is 1954. After working all day as a construction laborer, I stopped at Art Carroll's Grill for a few cold ones, and conversation with the regulars, which I was proud to be one of! There, at the bar, sat a guy I hadn't seen since high school – let's call him Jimmy Smith! Jimmy had been in the Army and had gone to Korea, as I had with the Marine Corps. He, too, was entering college in the fall.

One beer led to many more and Jimmy said, "Jack, guess who I'm going out with and sleeping with?" Before I could say a word he said, "Miss Doe!"

My heart rate tripled and I had to grab the bar before I fell off the stool – "Miss Doe!" I yelled, "You lucky bastard!"

Come to find out, Miss Doe was still teaching at the junior high and had never married. Jimmy had run into her at the A&P in Newton, and he asked her to lunch – the rest is history!

Jimmy Smith became a legend in my mind and in the mind of my friends. He cracked the code. He actually dated the teacher we were all in love with! He was a cult hero!

Just a little sidebar to this withdrawal from my Memory Bank. In 2002 through 2006, I read stories to kindergarten classes in Mayport, Florida at an elementary school. I believe the school went up to the fifth grade and then those kids went to middle school.

I firmly believe that kids fall in love with teachers at a younger age now. As I would walk through the school, I'd notice ten-year-old boys eyeing certain teachers with that "puppy love" stare. All was well with the world because boys and girls are still falling in love with their teachers.

FILENE'S BASEMENT

When my mother, Margaret Harrington, was a young girl, and before she married our father, she was an assistant buyer at Filene's Department Store in Boston. In 1908, Edward Filene, the son of the founder, opened Filene's Basement actually in the basement of the store at Downtown Crossing. They sold surplus goods, closeout merchandise, and called it the Automatic Bargain Basement, but everyone just called it The Basement. It became an institution in Boston, and in the 1940s, it enabled me and my two sisters to dress like millionaires for pennies on the dollar!

Our mother was a genius at finding the greatest looking items of clothing for next to nothing as she visited The Basement at least twice a week on her lunch break from the Boston Five Cent Savings Bank. She was friendly with some of the sales girls at The Basement, and they would put things aside for her to check out on a regular basis.

When I was discharged from the Marine Corps in 1953, all veterans in Massachusetts received a $300.00 bonus if you had served in the Korean War. Three-hundred bucks was a lot of money then, and I needed all new clothes. So off I went to The Basement!

I guess not too many twenty-two-year-old Marines ask their mother to take them shopping, but I visited The Basement with her on many occasions! A month after my discharge, we went to The Parker House for lunch and then to The Basement. I left there with an array of new clothes that would make Clark Gable, Humphrey Bogart, and Gregory Peck envious. I even had cashmere sweaters that we picked up for a dollar or two!

When you entered The Basement, manners and politeness were left at the door! It was a mad house. A faint-hearted shopper would never find a cashmere sweater for a buck. You had to fight your way to victory, and my mother had a gold medal in that area. Many a lunch we had at The Parker House where we went over our goals for the day at The Basement!

Never did we leave without both of us finding gems for ourselves and my sisters. Shopping at The Basement was an athletic competition, a battle of the fittest, and I was an amateur compared to my mother. It was great fun to see her in action and to be the junior part of the shopping team. Then on many a day, I'd take Mom to Bailey's for an ice cream sundae like we used to do after riding the Swan Boats when I was a kid.

Thanks Mom!

Dear Mom and Dad,

Although you haven't been by my side in person for quite a few years, you're always with me in spirit. Over the past couple of years, when writing up some of my withdrawals from my Memory Bank it's as though you've been sitting on my shoulders giving me inspiration.

Of course, all of the memories in this book wouldn't have been possible if you hadn't brought me into this world, so I thank you for doing just that. And, of course, thanks for doing the same for Sister and Julie. It wouldn't have been the same without them putting so many smiles in my Memory Bank!

I'll be eighty-years-old in December of this year. Of all the wonderful things you passed along to me over the years, one gift has come to the forefront often while going over my deposits in The Bank. You never burdened me, or my sisters, with the heavy weight of prejudice that many people carry with them all their lives. Since our normal way of life was to treat people with great respect, whatever their race, religion, or road they decided to follow, we naturally fell into step with you. If we had heard you belittle others when we were young, we would have missed out on a lot in this life.

I imagined, when arranging some of my withdrawals from The Bank, how lucky I am not to be loaded down with prejudice of any kind. After all, most kids turn out to be much like their parents in their thinking. So, thanks for allowing me to follow in your footsteps. I may have made a few bad turns in the road of life, and hit a few bumps, like most of us have, but what you passed along to me is priceless. How lucky I am!

Love,
Jack

Dear Sister,

As I checked out my balance sheet in my Memory Bank over the last couple of years, I realized that I needed an especially large safe deposit box for memories of you! I could write hundreds of pages in a separate book about you, and hardly a day ever goes by that I don't think of you.

Although you were born only fourteen months before I was, you were miles ahead of me in everything when I arrived in December of 1931. My very earliest memories of you always have to do with your watching out for me and teaching me the ropes of life.

The wonderful photo in my home office is of you and me sitting on a couch, and you have your arm around me. I think you're four-years-old and I'm three. It's easy to see by the smile on my face that you are the apple of my eye, and your smile says to me that you're glad I'm around.

Eight years ago today, St. Patrick's Day, you were with us in Florida to celebrate that day. We had just moved to Florida, and had put a new sunroom on the back of the house. You and Sally watched me out the window as I planted a Japanese maple tree. You each gave me hand signals as to which side of the tree to have facing the house, and you made sure I planted it straight.

The tree was only about six feet high and had a very thin trunk, but in eight years it's grown into a twenty-five or thirty-foot gem. The leaves are just coming out now, and "Sister's Tree" is blooming again. We see your tree everyday, and it brings a smile to our faces, just like our many thoughts of you do. Thanks, Sister, for being such a wonderful sister!

Love,
Jack

Dear Amy & Mark,

Last Friday at the Ace Hardware greenhouse sat a half dozen or so trumpet vine plants. It was as though the little orange trumpets blew in unison to call me over to their side! My thoughts quickly turned to your mother and our house in Newton Center in the early 1940's.

The small Victorian house on the hill at 112 Pleasant Street had the largest trumpet vine known to man or woman. It grew over the second story roof of the house and covered practically the whole side of the great little home. The vine, with its huge trunk and snake-like branches, always reminded Sister and me of the beanstalk that carried Jack to fame and fortune when he summoned up all his courage to make his famous climb!

Well, Sally and I untangled one of the plants from the other members of the brass section and rushed him home for planting! The next morning, feeling that he was lonesome, I went back and retrieved three of his friends to join him in our small yard. After all, one trumpet vine can't hit the high notes all alone, but four can jam with the best of them!

The vine in Newton Center played a not-so-small part in my early growth. My very small bedroom on the second floor had only one window, but what a wonderful window it was! One could practically walk through the open window without bending over and sit on a four-foot ledge to enjoy a clear New England night, while smoking a corncob pipe.

A ten or twelve-year-old would never waste money on store-bought tobacco when corn silk, ground up pine needles, or tea borrowed from the pantry was available! There is nothing quite like the delightful smell of pine needles and tea floating in the breeze that mixed with the aroma with that of the trumpets beside me at the great vantage point overlooking Pleasant Street.

For any agile kid, a trip up and down the trumpet vine was a piece of cake, and climbing in the dark just added an extra touch of excitement! Our detached garage, also known as The Coop was a special place to just hang out in like the chickens did in their coops. It was the perfect destination when the clock struck midnight. There was something terrific about a secret trip down the vine in the darkness, and one hundred feet away from the house could just as well have been New York City, Key West, or even the bleachers at Fenway Park!

Sister was only a little over a year older than me, but that's as close as I ever got to equalization! Her schoolwork was always honor roll level. She practically ran the household when she was eleven or twelve-years-old, and she seemed to have the eyes of an eagle and the hearing of a submarine's sonar system. So why would I ever have thought that my secret missions would go unnoticed?!

One morning, out of the blue, Sister smiled and said, "Jackie, you were a little noisier than usual climbing down the trumpet vine last night!"

I was speechless and in shock, and I could only muster, "What?"

"The trumpet vine…well you're becoming overconfident. In the beginning, you were very quiet, but now you can probably be heard all the way over to Crystal Lake!"

Denial never entered my mind when dealing with Sister. Anyone else, yes, but not Sister! "Ah, ah, ah, you're not going to tell Mom and Dad are ya?"

"I've thought about it, but I don't think so."

I continued my nighttime life, but not as frequently, and a little bit of the excitement rubbed off. Oh well, at least no one knew about my perch outside the window, where I could light up the corn silk, pine needles, and Lipton!

In a cigar box under my bed, I kept a few trinkets and a soap container that was the exact size of a cigarette pack. The pack of Lucky Strikes rested comfortably inside for extremely special occasions. On one of those rare occasions, a beautiful starry night on the roof was a perfect time to puff a Lucky.

Inside the soap box was a little note that said, "This ain't tea or corn silk!" Sister knew everything!!

Perhaps, in ten years I'll go out some evening, climb the trumpet vine up onto the porch roof and light up a pipe full of tea. At ninety years of age, I'll think it's tobacco, and that I might be putting one over on Sister…who, of course, is your mother!

Love,
Uncle Jack

Dear Julie,

It seems almost like yesterday that you arrived on the scene in Hingham, Massachusetts in 1937. I was six-years-old and Sister was seven. How lucky I was to now have two sisters!

My Memory Bank had been receiving deposits for quite a few years, and the day you came home from Massachusetts General Hospital is stamped on my entry file. There was great excitement on Free Street in Hingham, and that same excitement stayed with all of us during your life.

The Bank is filled with many Julie deposits, and I draw them out often. You had the greatest musical talent I ever saw, and you could play any song by ear at the drop of a hat. You started with classical music but branched out into everything else, including singing along with the tune. My very favorite was "Hurry On Down to My House Baby, There Ain't Nobody Home but Me!" Nellie Lutcher made that song famous, but Nellie had nothing on you.

Then, there was your uncanny ability of meeting someone for the first time, and in less than a half an hour, you knew their life history! Plus, it was instant friendship, and would remain so for life.

You, Julie, added a great deal to my life. Your pizzazz rubbed off on people, and I got more than my share of that from you. You left us all too early in life, but most people don't leave half the mark you made on people if they live to be one hundred. It was such fun having you as a sister. Thanks for making it so!

Love,
Jack

OUR KIDS

When an old-time person, like me, passes along so-called "words of wisdom" to some young kid – a grandson, granddaughter – whatever, it surely goes in one ear and out the other. Why shouldn't it? When I was, let's say fifteen, the passageway from one ear to the other was worn clean by all the suggestions and words of wisdom that rushed through the canal at breakneck speed never to be heard from again!

You can't tell anyone anything. They have to learn for themselves. Remember when you were eighteen and your grandmother or grandfather said, "Before you know it you'll be nearing the eighty-year-old mark wondering where all the years went!"

Hmmm…in December of 2011 I'll be eighty, and where the hell did all the years go? Gramp and Gram told me they'd fly by, but what did they know?

This year our son, Jack, will turn fifty-six. Bill will turn fifty-five. Stephen will turn fifty-four, my birthday present in December. Three boys in three years! Then, there is Wendy, the greatest surprise of our lives, who turns forty-five. Let me go on record and tell you that girls are easier to bring up than boys. I now know why my father was bald. He tore his hair out because of some of my escapades. I, too, am bald, but it happened much sooner for me. My father only had one son…I have three! But I wouldn't trade them in, no matter what the offer.

Since I've been spending quite a bit of time withdrawing deposits from my Memory Bank lately, I decided to pull one out at four o'clock this morning regarding our first house to call our own – well, ours and the other kind of bank! It ties right in with how time flies, for we've had a half dozen homes in later years.

We lived in a nice apartment in Newton, but with only two bedrooms and three kids, it was time to bite the bullet and try to come up with 5% down on a VA mortgage. We borrowed some money from our parents and went house hunting. We found a wonderful little bungalow on the Charles River for $15,500 with an extra lot on the river included!

It was one great place to live, and we spent two years there before we were transferred to the New York City area. We sold the house for $17,500 and the lot for $1,700, and we thought had hit the lottery. Perhaps some older person at the time told us to just keep the lot by the river, but if they did, it went in one ear and out the other as usual.

Over fifty years later we drove by our old neighborhood. Many of the small cottages were gone, and "McMansions" put up in their place.

A gentleman was putting out his trash barrel for pick up and I asked him a question. "Sir, how much is that house down the street that's for sale? Would you know?"

He told me it was on the market for $1,700,000! We told him our story about the lot we sold, and without missing a beat he said it would be worth way over a million now!

When we sold that lot, our income was $425.00 a month. A two-grand profit was almost a half a year's pay. But we sure wish we had kept that lot!

If there is any moral to this story, it has to be: When an older person gives you some advice, let it churn around in that canal between your two ears. Chances are the old timer who gave you the info is right!

Dear Jack, Billy, Stephen, and Wendy,

One of these years, maybe even in 2012, I'll draw some deposits out of my Memory Bank that have been gaining interest all these years. I could surely fill a thick book with those withdrawals about you guys.

My wonderful father lost his hair because of some of the shenanigans I pulled when I was young. However, what goes around comes around, and I, too, lost my hair early in life with the help of you guys! However, 90% of the loss is blamed on you boys – only 10% came out by Wendy's doing. But I wouldn't have it any other way! Each morning while shaving, I smile into the mirror thinking of deposits of all of you in The Bank.

We've sure had some fun, and your mother and I are proud of all of you. There are deposits in The Bank for Jack's wonderful friend, Diane, for Billy's great wife, Katie, and their kids Mike and Megan, along with Donna, Stephen's wife, and Danny, their son.

All of my nieces and nephews are in The Bank, and Sally's sister, Betsi and husband, Rob, and their great kids Kim and Beck.

I'm hoping to live to be at least ninety so I can continue my withdrawals of you kids, along with many friends I haven't mentioned.

Love & Happy Days,
Dad

Dear Sally,

Much has happened since we were married in September of 1954, a day or so after Hurricane Carol. No electricity in the church, but the candlelight was much nicer than the bright lights, and with no electricity, the organist couldn't play "Here Comes the Bride." But you know, we were able to generate our own electricity for the last fifty-seven yours, and I see no reason why we can't continue to generate power for at least another ten or fifteen!

Over a lifetime we all encounter bumps in the road, but when we did, we always seemed to get back on the smooth highway soon. Thanks for taking this long ride with me, and let's continue to stay on the bus until the last stop. The ride has been great, and although the bus doesn't go as fast anymore, it's still running! See you on the bus!

Much love,
Jack

A LIFE CHANGING DEPOSIT

Every deposit in your Memory Bank isn't the peaches and cream variety. All of us have an area in the vault that holds a safe deposit box containing sad memories. We don't seem to withdraw them anywhere near as often as the happier deposits, but from time to time, they come out for review.

There is one deposit in The Bank that began as a no-interest entry, and thankfully, it ended up at the top of my portfolio. It's classified and filed away as life-changing. It wasn't deposited until I was forty-eight years old, but it increased in value faster than most!

When I look back, my problem with alcohol started at a young age and progressed from there. Since the alcoholic is the last one to know that they actually are one, it usually takes many years before you're forced to confront the disease. From my Marine Corps days, right up to 1980, my battle with alcohol was never-ending. I functioned well enough to be successful in the business world, but there were many bumps in the road along the way.

In late 1979, I was at the end of my rope. I still couldn't admit to myself that alcohol was the problem, and surely I had no thought of getting sober. However, I was having real problems with my job and had considered suicide at various times. It all crashed down on me one long weekend and my wife, Sally, knew something had to be done or something drastic would happen. She called my great friend Bob White in Connecticut late one night, and he called me the next morning at seven o'clock.

Bob worked with me in the same publishing company, and we were close friends. I never knew Bob to even take a drink, but my only thought was that he just didn't like it. It never entered my mind that he was a recovering alcoholic. Bob is no longer alive, but if he were, he wouldn't mind my mentioning him by name as being in recovery.

Bob would call me every week or so just to say hello and to see how I was doing. I realized later on that he knew damn well that I was in deep trouble with booze, and only wanted to help me if he could.

When Bob called, I was sick as a dog with a hangover of giant proportions. When he asked me how I was doing, I tried to fake it and told him I was getting ready to head up to Boston to the office. Then it hit me like a runaway Mack truck. I started to cry uncontrollably. He calmed me down and said he had to be in New York for the day and he couldn't change his plans, but would be at our house the next morning. He told me to try to not drink that day, but if I couldn't do that not to worry about it, just stay home.

A half-hour later I had a call from another close friend from work, Frank Mitchell, whom Bob had called. Frank appeared a couple of hours later, and we went out to lunch. Somehow, I didn't drink at lunch and was able to continue that for the whole day.

The next morning, after a three-hour drive, Bob White knocked on our door at seven o'clock! We had coffee, we talked, and we talked. Around nine he said, "Jack, get cleaned up, and we're going to a meeting!"

I panicked, "What kind of a meeting?"

"An AA meeting in Plymouth."

Then, I double-panicked and told him I couldn't go. When he asked why, I said, "I can't. What happens if I see someone I know there?"

I'll never forget the look on Bob's face as he laughed and said, "Just say 'Hi, how ya doing.'" Of course, thinking back, that was a dumb thing for me to say. If I saw someone I knew they were there for the same reason I was – because they wanted to get sober!

I had the shakes and not from just being nervous. I was in big-time withdrawal. The room in Memorial Hall in Plymouth had about thirty guys there from all walks of life. Bob took me over to a coffee urn where everyone filled up their cup and sat down for the meeting.

Just before a speaker got up to talk, a guy turned around and looked at me as he said, "Jack, am I glad to see you here!"

I was shocked. He was a good friend of mine, younger than me, that I had played tennis tournaments with as doubles partners. We had won tournaments together, and it never entered my mind that Phil had a drinking problem. I thought that, like Bob, Phil just didn't care for booze! He told me to call him any time of day if I wanted advice or a helping hand, and two complete strangers said the same things he had. Maybe I had come to the right place.

Bob spent the day with me and urged me to attend ninety AA meetings in ninety days, or even double meetings a day at times. I had to "dry out," but I didn't go to a rehab. I did it at home and went to meetings. I took two weeks off from work to concentrate on not drinking.

At the meetings, I listened to every speaker, but in the back of my mind was the recurring thought that I'd be able to drink socially after a few months. I mean, how could I ever do business without drinking? I'd have a few drinks a day, and control it with no problem. However, as they say in AA meetings, "Keep on coming." And I did, and I didn't drink.

Then, one night out of left field came a true life changing bolt out of the blue. A speaker got up and said, "Hi, my name is George and I'm an alcoholic. It's nice to be here and nice to be sober.

I said to myself, *I know, but soon I can drink again socially.*

219

Then George said, "But more than that, it's nice to know that I don't have to drink anymore!"

Well, it was as though someone hit me over the head with a club. It was as though George was talking directly to me, and the message exploded with great joy throughout my whole body...I didn't have to drink anymore!

When I got home, Sally asked her usual question, "How was the meeting?"

I told her a miracle had happened when George literally imbedded those six words in my mind, "I DON'T HAVE TO DRINK ANYMORE!"

Months before, when Bob White visited me, Sally supported me in many ways, one of which was to join me in not drinking. I couldn't have stayed sober without her help.

From that day on, I never had to make excuses for not having a drink at the tennis club or anywhere else. I didn't have to tell so-called friends that I was on medication and couldn't drink for a while. I could tell the world I was a recovering alcoholic, and I didn't drink, and didn't give a damn who knew it.

I've met a lot of people in my life, but none more helpful than those I met in AA. Thanks to Bob White, Phil, my wife, Sally, Jimmy and many others, I was put on the path to sobriety, which is the best path I've ever traveled. So you see, I'm always glad to draw January 12, 1980, out of my Memory Bank! It was the beginning of a new life for my family and me.

Over the years, I've passed along to others, what Bob White gave me. That, of course, means that Bob has continued to help people through the guy he saved those many years ago.

THANKS FOR LISTENING

A few years ago, when I began fooling around with writing down my Memory Bank withdrawals for our kids to check out, I realized I had great fun doing it. Then I read a few of them to senior groups in Florida, and they enjoyed them to the point where a few suggested I put them in book form. My next question was, "Would you buy this book if I had it with me?" When a group of about 150 people raised their hands with a rousing, "Yes!" I thought maybe I could actually sell some books and make deposits in my other bank!

Of course, I also thought that it was easy to say, "Yeah, we'll buy your book" when I didn't have any with me! Well, if you're reading this, thank you. You must have bought my book, and I appreciate it. In 2004, I self-published another book entitled, *I Can't Hear You!* It's about a kid (me) and his three years in the Marine Corps. Those who read it, liked it, but I never really marketed the book. I plan to promote *The Memory Bank* on a larger scale, if possible. So, if you enjoyed the book, please tell your friends about it. If you didn't, please *don't* tell your friends about it!

I'm beginning to draw out deposits that have been in my account since the 50s, 60s and 70s, so you may be hearing from me again when I'm eighty- two or so! Once again, thanks for listening!

Happy Days – Jack Orth

ABOUT THE AUTHOR

Jack Orth was born in Boston, Massachusetts in 1931. He served in the U.S. Marine Corps and is a decorated Marine from the Korean War.

He attended Boston University and enjoyed a long career in business-to-business publishing in advertising sales. For many years, he wrote a column for New England Advertising Week called "Unorthodox by Jack," as well as business newsletters and guest columns in Marine Corps Publications.

He and his wife, Sally, are retired in Jacksonville, Florida. They have four children and three grandchildren.